The Book of
SAINTS

A NOTE TO THE TEXT

The saints featured in the main body of this book are presented chronologically. The list of their feast days is not exhaustive, as some have more than one feast day or are commemorated on different days in different calendars.

In the interests of clarity, a country such as Gaul is called by its modern name, France.

Where the exact date of the window is not known, "c." before a date in the caption indicates an approximate date, while "m." before one indicates the memorial date on the window. The memorial date invariably gives the year of death of the person in whose memory the window is given but there was often a lapse of some years (as much as twenty) before the installation. It is important to bear this in mind if trying to build up a picture of the developing style of a particular artist or studio.

PHOTOGRAPHY Copyright © Sonia Halliday and Laura Lushington
ADDITIONAL PHOTOGRAPHY pp. 12, 13, 24, 27,
43, 55, 57, 75, 79, 92, 99, 143: copyright © David Lawrence
pp. 67, 108: copyright © Washington National Cathedral
p. 64: copyright © Quadrillion Publishing with special thanks to All Saints' Church, Selsley
EDITOR Fleur Robertson
DESIGNER Louise Clements
PRODUCTION Neil Randles, Karen Staff, Ruth Arthur
DIRECTOR OF PRODUCTION Graeme Procter

5074 The Book of Saints
Copyright © 1998 Quadrillion Publishing Ltd.
Published in 1998 by CLB, an imprint of Quadrillion Publishing Ltd,
Godalming, Surrey, GU7 1XW, England
Distributed in the U.S.A. by Quadrillion Publishing Inc.
203 Fifth Avenue, New York, NY 10001

Printed and bound in Singapore
ISBN 1-85833-396-2

Previous page: The Ascension,
William Morris, Morris & Co., 1861-2, All Saints' Church, Selsley, Gloucestershire, England
These pages: main picture: Bernard (page 114-15)
inset: Bartholomew (page 40-41)

The Book of
SAINTS

Lesley Whiteside

PHOTOGRAPHY
Sonia Halliday and Laura Lushington

ADDITIONAL PHOTOGRAPHY
David Lawrence

Contents

The Martyrdom of Sebastian, *c.1280, Freiburg Cathedral, Germany*

Introduction

IN ONE VERY significant sense, all who serve God are saints, for the word means "made holy" or "set apart for God." This was the usage in the early church, as, for example, in Paul's greeting to "The church of God … in Corinth, to those who are sanctified in Christ Jesus, called to be saints." (1 Cor. 1:2) However, when we talk about a "saint" today, we usually mean an outstanding Christian.

The first saints of this type were the martyrs of the early church. The Christian community venerated the places where martyrs died and were buried, treasured their relics, invoked their help, observed the anniversary of their death, and eventually dedicated churches to them. During the fourth century imperial persecution of the church ended and gradually the term "saint" was extended to people of exemplary devotion—ascetics such as Antony the hermit, teachers such as Basil, and bishops such as Ambrose—who bore witness to the gospel not necessarily in their death but in their lives and were thus called "confessors."

Over the centuries the number of saints grew and continues to grow in the closing years of the second millennium, as believers in some countries still die for their faith and the lives of others provide truly inspiring examples of the Christian life in a secular world—Janani Luwum and Oscar Romero among the former, Mother Teresa and Gladys Aylward among the latter. Very few of these are officially canonized, but are remembered on All Saints' Day with the great multitude "who worship on another shore and in a greater light."

Visitors to a church may appreciate the stained glass purely for its aesthetic function of introducing light and color to the building, but its spiritual ▷

The Martyrs' Window, c.1280, Freiburg Cathedral, Germany

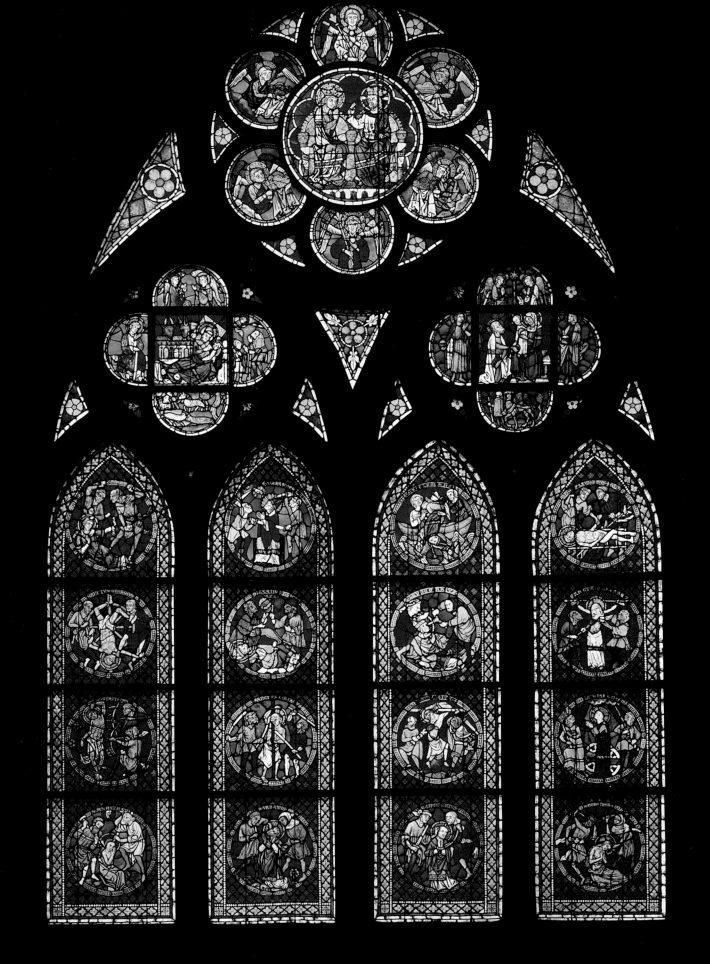

dimension is far greater: It builds on the image of God as the light of the world and adds to the sense of the numinous. It is a powerful devotional aid.

The art of stained glass developed throughout the medieval period and reached its zenith in Gothic Europe from the late twelfth until the fourteenth century. After several centuries of decline, the nineteenth-century Gothic revival brought a new flowering of the art. In Britain particularly there was a great spate of church building, and while Victorian glass is often derided as dull and repetitive in design, the best is very good.

Several factors make it difficult to appreciate medieval windows fully: they have been keeping out the elements for a very long time and all show some signs of wear and tear. Many have suffered a serious loss of paint, while others have suffered at the hands of inept restorers. (Happily, there are some excellent restorers, as can be seen in some of the windows in this book.) Another factor is the need to decipher the complex signs and symbols which would have met with instant recognition then but with which we are unfamiliar. I have tried to interpret as many of these as space permits, in the hope that it will encourage readers to go to churches and look at the glass with more appreciative eyes.

In a book of this size about the saints, there is inevitably a high degree of selectivity. By and large, the saints seen in stained glass are the biblical and early saints, but I have tried to maintain a balance between them and the medieval and modern saints. Representations of modern saints are few and their omission is not intended to diminish them—I would have liked to have included an illustration of Maximilian Kolbe, for example, but one wasn't available. Although the photographers have traveled far and wide to take the photographs in this book, most of the windows are in England, Ireland, France, or Germany; readers may find excellent stained-glass depictions of the saints nearer home.

The Adoration of the Magi and Shepherds, *Douglas Strachan, 1931, Church of St. Thomas, Winchelsea, East Sussex, England*

9

The Four Evangelists

THE NEW TESTAMENT, particularly the four gospels and the Acts of the Apostles, is the source of our knowledge about Christ, his mother, and the apostles. None of the gospel writers identifies himself by name, but the traditions attributing them to Matthew, Mark, Luke, and John go back at least as far as the second century. The window overleaf gives a thrilling modern presentation of the traditional symbols of the four evangelists, grouped around Christ in glory. These symbols, all winged creatures, reflect what was considered to be the emphasis of each gospel: for Matthew, a man symbolizing Christ's humanity; for Mark, a lion symbolizing his kingship; for Luke, an ox symbolizing his sacrificial priesthood, while an eagle stands for John, who "soars to heaven."

Meg Lawrence's assured draughtmanship and bold coloration gives a lively impression of the gospels, with an energetic young man, a regal lion, patient ox, and majestic eagle. That Matthew based his Gospel on the earlier Mark's Gospel is suggested by the fact that the man is stretching his hand out toward the lion.

Mark's Gospel has particular importance as the earliest (probably written about 70), and as the basis of the other synoptic gospels of Matthew and Luke. It is even more significant if, as has always been thought, it reflects Peter's account. Mark was not an apostle, but his Gospel reads very much like a first-hand account and is a brief, urgent, no-frills narrative, just as Peter would have given. Significantly, the narrative ignores Christ's birth and youth and begins with his baptism, just before he commenced his ministry.

Matthew's Gospel, its narrative carefully linked to the Old Testament prophecies, addresses Christ's Jewishness. Thus it begins by tracing Christ's genealogy back to Abraham and gives an elaborate account of his birth. Its highly organized teaching sections ensured its use as a manual of Christian instruction, though it lacks the urgency of Mark and the feeling of Luke.

Luke sets out his objectives in the first verses of his Gospel. Writing for a believer called Theophilus, he refers to other accounts of Christ's life and death and says, "I decided, after investigating everything carefully, to write an orderly account for you, so that you may know the truth concerning the things about which you have been instructed." (Luke 1:3-4) Luke's message is clear and compelling: Christ fulfils the Old Testament prophecies of the Messiah and is the friend and savior of people of every race and condition. Luke tells the parables of the lost coin and the prodigal son to convey "the joy" in heaven "over one sinner who repents." (Luke 15:10) He also stresses the happiness of the Christian, ending his gospel with the apostles returning to Jerusalem after the Ascension "with great joy."

The different emphasis of John's Gospel is clear from the first verses: "In the beginning was the Word and the Word was with God, and the Word was God." Meg Lawrence's magnificent eagle suggests the mystery and theological complexities that permeate John's Gospel. It includes some of the most difficult sayings of Jesus, but also those which over the centuries have proved such a source of strength: "I am the bread of life, … the light of the world, … the good shepherd, … the true vine … the way, the truth and the life."

Christ Enthroned,
with the Symbols
of the Evangelists,
Meg Lawrence, 1995,
Church of St. John
the Evangelist,
Brownswood Park, London

The Blessed Virgin Mary

THE ANNUNCIATION

March 25

IN ONE RESPECT Mary and the apostles are the core of this book but this is true only because of their relationship to Jesus Christ himself. For this reason, the book begins with a window depicting the announcement of his forthcoming birth. William Morris's cinquefoil depicts the angel Gabriel appearing to tell Mary she will conceive by the Holy Spirit a son who will be called Son of God.

The gospels are not interested in Mary herself but as the woman chosen by God as the mother of the Messiah. Nevertheless, we can build a picture from Luke's account. Mary clearly was an innocent and devout young girl, looking forward to a respectable marriage to Joseph the carpenter, when Gabriel came with his extraordinary news. This spelt rejection by Joseph and disgrace in Jewish society, but, in faith, Mary replied: "Here am I, the servant of the Lord; let it be with me according to your word." (Luke 1:38) Her faith was justified when God reassured Joseph they should marry as planned.

Mary's considered response to Gabriel's news is a song of praise known as the Magnificat. It begins with the words: "My soul magnifies the Lord, and my spirit rejoices in God my Saviour, for he has looked with favour on the lowliness of his servant." (Luke 1:46-8)

The Annunciation, *William Morris, Morris & Co., 1880, All Saints' Church, Middleton Cheney, Buckinghamshire, England*

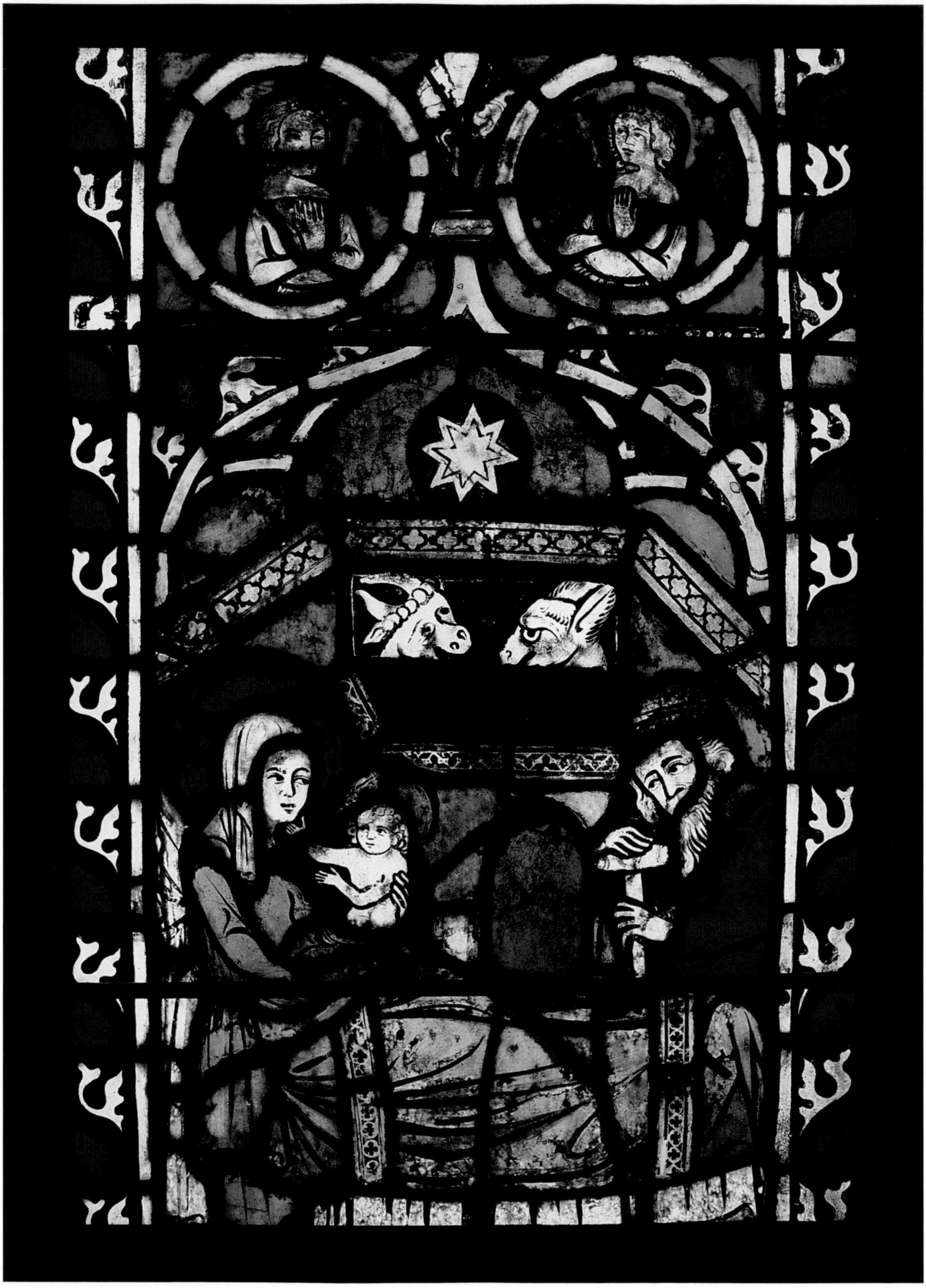

The Blessed Virgin Mary

THE NATIVITY

THE NATIVITY AND the Adoration are commemorated in Christian art of every age. The panel opposite show the intimacy of the Nativity in the manger. Mary holds the infant Jesus in her arms, while Joseph kneels beside them. Their joy is matched by the joyful faces of the ox and ass in the background! In contrast, Douglas Strachan's "Adoration of the Magi and Shepherds" (p. 8) emphasises Mary's dignity and the solemnity of the occasion, by using an intense blue for Mary's robes and combining that steely blue with other metallic shades throughout the scene. The intensity of expression and body language of wise man and shepherd alike leaves no doubt of the momentous significance of the Nativity.

We should never cease to be amazed that, as the English poet Sir John Betjeman (1903-1990) put it, "God was man in Palestine." The Incarnation is explained in John1:14: "The Word became flesh and lived among us, and we have seen his glory, the glory as of a father's only son, full of grace and truth."

There is no mention in the Bible of Mary's parents. An early apocryphal writing, which sought to give an account of Mary's origins, named them as Joachim and Ann. Later, as the cult of Mary grew, so did the cult of "Ann, Mother of our Lady," and a great number of churches were dedicated to her.

The Nativity, *fourteenth century, Church of St. Étienne, Mulhouse, France*

✠

The Blessed Virgin Mary

THE PIETÀ

HERE IS VERY little mention of Mary after Jesus reached the age of twelve until she stood at the foot of the cross. Then Christ, in his own agony, recognized *her* suffering and entrusted her to the care of John (p. 34). Although there is no specific mention of Mary at the deposition and burial of Christ, it is reasonable to assume that she was involved. The Pietà (representation of Mary holding the body of the crucified Christ) is a frequent subject of paintings, sculpture, and stained glass. It is often as moving an image of the Passion as a representation of the Crucifixion itself. Although the St. Neot Pietà, in Cornwall, England, was beautifully renewed in the nineteenth century, the figure of Christ shows a lot of wear and tear, so there is an almost unbearable symbolism in the twice-broken body of our Lord.

After the Ascension, Mary and some other women watched and prayed with the apostles. She may have been with them on the day of Pentecost, when they were all filled with the Holy Spirit. Nothing more is known about Mary but a considerable cult grew round her. As the mother of the Lord, she is a very special figure in both the Catholic and Orthodox traditions. In Poland, for example, she is venerated as "Mary, Queen of Poland," a title which conveys her unique appeal to many.

The Pietà, *late fifteenth century (restored, c.1830 by J.H. Nixon, artist, and J.P. Hedgeland, architect), Church of St. Anietus, St. Neot, Cornwall, England*

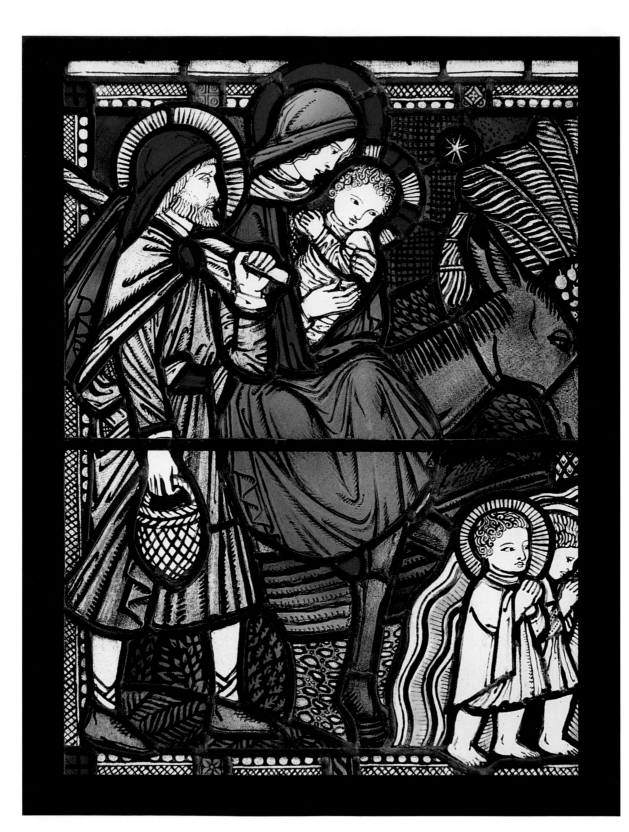

Joseph

March 19/May 1

JOSEPH, THE HUSBAND of the Virgin Mary, is revered for his role as Christ's foster-father. Although the gospel writers are at pains to establish the virgin birth, they point out Joseph was of the royal house of David and in all other instances refer to him as Christ's father. He was present at Christ's birth and at all the significant stages of his early life.

An angel appeared to Joseph at certain vital moments, first to reassure him it was right to marry Mary, as her baby was the child of the Holy Spirit; later to urge him to take Mary and Jesus to Egypt to avoid Herod's slaughter of the Holy Innocents; later again, after Herod's death, to return to Galilee. Joseph's dependability is suggested in this window by Hendrie's strength of line and bold brushwork, showing him striding out beside Mary and Jesus, yet intimately grouped with them. (A fascinating representation of the Holy Innocents shows them as two tiny figures, closely watched by the infant Jesus.)

Joseph is the model of the caring father and an exceptional example of a man putting the interests of his wife before his own. The first of May, the feast day of Joseph the carpenter, serves as a useful reminder of the value and dignity of manual labor. Again and again in the gospel narrative it is clear God chooses the humble and lowly as his instruments.

The Flight to Egypt, *Herbert Hendrie, c.1921, Church of St. Peter Mancroft, Norwich, England*

Elizabeth

November 5

ALL WE KNOW about Elizabeth, the mother of John the Baptist, is derived from Luke. He begins his gospel with the prophecy of John's birth. Elizabeth, a descendant of Aaron, was married to a priest called Zechariah, with whom she shares a feast day. They were a devout and aging couple, who had no children. Zechariah was absolutely incredulous when the angel Gabriel appeared to tell him that Elizabeth was going to bear a son called John, who would "make ready a people prepared for the Lord." Because of his doubts, he lost his power of speech.

When Elizabeth received a visit from Mary, she was filled with the Holy Spirit. Recognizing the young cousin who had come to visit her as "the mother of my Lord," she exclaimed, "Blessed are you among women, and blessed is the fruit of your womb." This dignified portrayal of the Visitation conveys Elizabeth's sense of awe.

Elizabeth duly gave birth to her son and, when Zechariah had written the name "John" on a tablet, he recovered his speech and gave the prophecy known as the Benedictus. In it he celebrated his son as "the prophet of the Most High; for you will go before the Lord to prepare his ways, to give knowledge of salvation to his people by the forgiveness of their sins." (Luke 1:5-79)

The Visitation, *1440, Church of St. Peter Mancroft, Norwich, England*

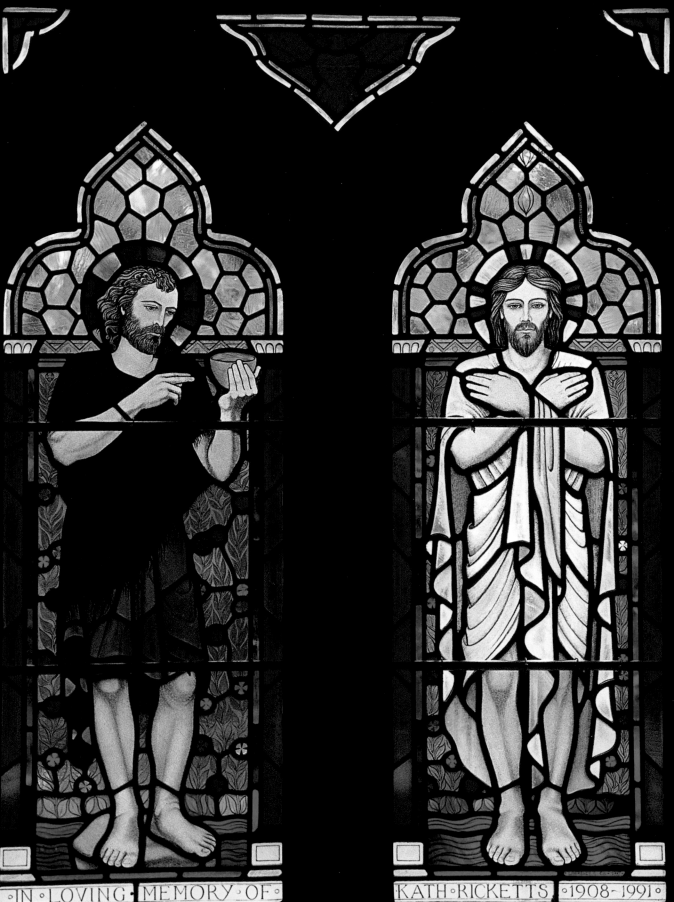

IN·LOVING·MEMORY·OF· KATH·RICKETTS·1908-1991

John the Baptist

June 24

W HILE MOST MODERN stained glass tends toward the abstract, Meg Lawrence's drawing of John the Baptist is simple and strong and thus powerfully conveys this rugged character. The bowl cupped in his hand emphasises his ministry as baptiser of Jesus, who is shown receiving the Holy Spirit (represented in the tracery by a dove, whose feathers merge into Pentecostal tongues of flame).

Bridging the gap between Old Testament prophet and Christian disciple, John himself fulfilled Isaiah's prophecy of "the voice … crying in the wilderness: 'Prepare the way of the Lord.'" (Isa. 40:3) He lived an austere life (Matthew records John's food was locusts and wild honey), preached a baptism of repentance and proclaimed the coming of the Messiah.

John was an outspoken critic of the Jewish establishment—"you brood of vipers!" he called some Pharisees and Sadducees—and his forthright denunciation of Herod Antipas for marrying his brother's wife, Herodias, led to his execution. Having imprisoned John to silence him, Herod found himself obliged to execute him to fulfil a promise to Herodias's daughter to give her anything she asked. At her mother's prompting, Salome demanded the head of John the Baptist. Thus died the prophet of whom Jesus said: "Among those born of women no one is greater than John." (Luke 7:28)

The Baptism of Christ, Meg Lawrence, 1997, Church of St. John the Baptist, Cookham Dean, Berkshire, England

Andrew

November 30

GALILEAN FISHERMEN, ANDREW and his brother, Simon Peter, were the first disciples whom Jesus called. One day they were casting their nets into the water when Jesus came along and said: "Follow me and I will make you fish for people." (Mark 1:16-18) They did this at once, thus beginning a life of discipleship and service. This redirection from fishing for food to fishing for people is a reminder that Christ addresses people as they are and draws on their existing skills in his service.

John's Gospel gives Andrew particular importance as the first follower of Jesus. He says Andrew was a disciple of John the Baptist until John pointed out Christ to him as the Messiah. After seeking out Christ and spending a day with him, Andrew was convinced and persuaded Peter to come and see for himself. This must have happened before their calling.

Andrew's eager response to Christ's call is vividly captured in this early window by Clayton and Bell, who were in the forefront of the English stained-glass revival in the nineteenth century. Their early work, seen here in the style of the late fourteenth century, is noted for its vitality and rich coloration.

We have no idea what happened to Andrew in later life and the suggestion he died on an X-shaped cross is a late one. He is the patron saint of Russia, Greece, and Scotland.

The Call of Andrew, *Clayton & Bell, m.1863, Church of St. Andrew, Kilmurry, Co. Cork, Ireland*

Peter

THE WASHING OF THE FEET

June 29

ETER IS THE most lovable and inspiring of the apostles, a person with whom we readily identify. Originally called Simon, Christ gave him the name "Peter" (meaning "Rock"), saying, "You are Peter, and on this rock I will build my church, and the gates of Hades will not prevail against it. I will give you the keys of the kingdom of heaven, and whatever you bind on earth will be bound in heaven." (Matt. 16:18-19)

Christ clearly recognized Peter's wholehearted, loving commitment and his ability to lead. It was these qualities, not his intellectual powers, which made him a towering figure among the twelve. Indeed, he was ruled by his heart rather than his head, a spontaneous and impulsive man. The famous incident illustrated here in the Passion and Resurrection window in Chartres Cathedral shows this endearing aspect of Peter. At the Last Supper, Christ knelt to wash the disciples' feet. Peter, horrified that his Lord should undertake this lowly service, said, "You will never wash my feet." When Christ replied, 'Unless I wash you, you have no share with me," Peter cried, "Lord, not my feet only but also my hands and my head!" (John 13:2-10) This is the moment captured here. Not for the first time, Peter had got it wrong and was gently rebuked. It reminds us every disciple must begin by letting Christ serve him or her.

Christ Washing Peter's Feet, twelfth century, Chartres Cathedral, France

PETER

THE DENIAL

CHRIST THEN TOLD the disciples about his imminent betrayal, prompting Peter to vow that he would die for his sake. Christ, however, warned: "Before the cock crows, you will have denied me three times." (John 13:38) After Christ's arrest, when the disciples fled in fear, Peter followed him to the high priest's house. Acker shows the first of Peter's denials, on being questioned by a servant-girl in the courtyard. His additional denials are suggested by Peter's dejected posture and the vigilant cock.

Yet, we can find encouragement in this devastating incident, for Peter, having failed so badly, had his commission renewed by Christ after the Resurrection. There is hope for every struggling Christian. After the Ascension Peter lived up to his responsibilities as the leader of the church. It was he who addressed the crowd on the day of Pentecost, he who first admitted a Gentile to the Christian community. He healed so many people that the sick were laid in the streets for his shadow to fall on them.

Some of his teaching is reported at length in Acts, more in 1 Peter. While it is unlikely he wrote 2 Peter, it is generally believed he was the chief source for Mark's gospel. There is a very strong tradition (largely confirmed by modern scholars) that Peter was the first leader of the church in Rome and that he was martyred there about A.D. 64.

Peter's Denial, *Hans Acker, c.1430 (reconstructed by Hans Gottfried von Stockhausen, 1964-5),*
Ulm Cathedral, Germany

James the Great

July 25

JAMES AND HIS brother, John, the sons of Zebedee, were also called from a life of fishing. Clearly they and Peter had some precedence among the apostles, for they were chosen to be with Christ at certain crucial moments. In Chartres their depiction at the Transfiguration is inspired by earlier Byzantine art. Christ, lit by eight spokes of light, is the central figure. Moses and Elijah, representing the Law and Prophecy, which are fulfilled in Christ, stand on each side of him. James (right), John (center), and Peter (left) hear a voice saying, "This is my Son, the Beloved," and fall to the ground in fear. (Matt 17:1-8)

Christ's nickname for them, "Sons of Thunder," suggests the brothers were difficult colleagues. The tensions caused by their request to sit beside him in glory are a reminder the church has always accommodated people who bring their gifts *and* imperfections to the community. Altered and matured by the Passion, Resurrection, and Pentecost, their perspective changed from preoccupation with their own status to spreading the good news of Christ risen, ascended and glorified. James was the first apostle to be martyred, on the orders of Herod Agrippa about A.D. 44. According to medieval legend, James evangelized Spain and his relics were taken to Compostela.

The Transfiguration, *twelfth century, Chartres Cathedral, France*

John the Evangelist

December 27

I F JOHN, IN old age, used a scribe to write his version of the gospel, it is not surprising he is referred to, not by name, but as "the disciple whom Jesus loved." Opposite is Burne-Jones's rendering of John's account of the Crucifixion: "Standing near the cross of Jesus were his mother, and his mother's sister, Mary the wife of Clopas, and Mary Magdalene. When Christ saw his mother and the disciple he loved standing beside her, he said: 'Woman, here is your son.' Then he said to the disciple: 'Here is your mother.' And from that hour the disciple took her into his own home." (John 19:25-7) It is notable that Christ showed great faith in John by entrusting her to his care.

On hearing from Mary Magdalene that the tomb was empty, John ran there "and saw and believed." (John 20:8) The realisation Christ had risen from the dead began a transformation in the apostles which prepared them for their empowerment at Pentecost. In this "Son of Thunder," personal ambition was replaced by God-given authority. It seems likely John spent his last years at Ephesus, where he established a "school" of thinkers, but it is uncertain whether he or one of his followers wrote the Epistles of John and Revelation.

The Crucifixion, *Edward Burne-Jones, Morris & Co., 1885, All Hallows' Church, Allerton, Liverpool, England*

Thomas

July 3

THOMAS, ALSO CALLED "Didymus" (the twin), is universally known as "doubting Thomas." We can all identify with Thomas in his doubts and benefit from the response they elicited.

Thomas was not present when Christ appeared to the disciples after the Resurrection. Not daring to believe what the others told him, he argued that he would have to see the nail marks and feel the wounds before he believed that Christ had risen. A week later, Christ appeared again and immediately said to Thomas: "Put your finger here and see my hands. Reach out your hand and put it in my side. Do not doubt but believe." This window illustrates the point at which Thomas reaches out and cries, "My Lord and my God!" Christ's response has encouraged Christians throughout the centuries: "Blessed are those who have not seen and yet have come to believe." (John 20: 25-9)

An earlier incident reveals the same doubting Thomas: during the Last Supper, Christ was trying to reassure his disciples, despite his imminent betrayal and death, all would be well. "I go to prepare a place for you," he told them. "And you know the way to the place where I am going." Thomas immediately said: "Lord, we do not know where you are going. How can we know the way?" Then came the great reply: "I am the way, and the truth, and the life." (John 14: 2-7)

"Doubting" Thomas, *sixteenth century, Church of St. Pierre, Dreux, France*

Matthew

September 21

THE CALL OF Matthew (also called Levi) to be a disciple was much more dramatic than that of the fishermen, for he was a tax collector, one of a group despised for their dishonest methods. He was actually seated at his tax booth when Christ walked past. The gospel account is frustratingly succinct, saying only that Jesus "saw" Matthew and "said to him, 'Follow me.' And he got up and followed him." (Matt. 9:9)

Matthew's recruitment shows Christ did not choose only the respectable for leadership. This point is reinforced by an altercation at the banquet which Matthew held at his house in honor of Christ. Predictably, the Pharisees were scandalized that Christ should eat with "tax collectors and sinners" and their criticism prompted the reply: "Those who are well have no need of a physician, but those who are sick … I have come to call not the righteous but sinners." (Matt. 9:12-13)

The last mention of Matthew in the New Testament is of his presence as one of the remaining eleven apostles at the Ascension and Pentecost, when they received the power of the Holy Spirit. While scholars are not convinced Matthew was the author of the gospel which bears his name, nor that Mark, Luke, and John, who feature in the early church, wrote the other gospels, such doubts do not diminish either the gospels or the historical figures.

Matthew, Lorin of Chartres, 1888, Church of St. Aignan, Chartres, France

Bartholomew

August 24

T IS GENERALLY accepted that Bartholomew, the apostle, is the same person as Nathanael. While the synoptic gospels list the twelve as Peter, Andrew, the brothers James and John, Philip, Bartholomew, Thomas, Matthew, James, son of Alphaeus, Jude/Thaddaeus, Simon, and Judas Iscariot, John makes no mention of Bartholomew but lists Nathanael as one of those to whom the risen Lord appeared at the Sea of Galilee. The way in which John writes of Nathanael leaves no doubt that he was an apostle, so we have to assume he was more frequently called Bartholomew.

John says when Philip recruited Nathanael, Christ greeted him by saying: "Here is truly an Israelite in whom there is no guile." In amazement, Nathanael asked how Christ knew him. Christ's reply, "I saw you under the fig tree before Philip called you," was enough to prompt a profession of faith from Nathanael, showing that he was indeed a guileless man. (John 1:43-9)

This is exactly the Bartholomew portrayed here (in the tracery of the west window of Canterbury Cathedral), with an open face, a gentle and pensive expression. In his right hand he holds a butcher's knife, which symbolizes his martyrdom. He is said to have taken the gospel to Armenia, there to have been flayed alive, but there is no proof of this tradition.

Bartholomew, *late fourteenth century, reworked, Canterbury Cathedral, England*

Philip and James, Son of Alphaeus

May 1/May 3

A S THE REMAINING apostles are not depicted individually, this illustration of the feeding of the five thousand has been chosen to represent their ministry in general and Philip and James in particular. When Jesus gave the twelve their commission, he sent them out to proclaim the gospel, to heal the sick, and to minister to the needy.

Faced with a large crowd, who had followed him up a mountainside, Jesus knew he must feed them. To "test" Philip, he asked him, "Where are we going to buy bread for these people?" Philip replied, "Six months' wages would not buy enough bread for each of them to get a little." While Philip could not suggest a solution, Andrew pointed to a boy with five barley loaves and two fishes, adding, "But what are they among so many people?" Jesus told the apostles to make the people sit down. Then he took and blessed this small offering and the disciples were able to distribute more than enough for everyone to eat! (John 6:1-14)

Tradition identifies James the son of Alphaeus with James "the less" and James "the brother of the Lord," writer of the Epistle but, in reality, we know nothing more about James the son of Alphaeus.

The Feeding of the Five Thousand, *Lavers, Barraud & Westlake, 1882,*
Church of the Ascension, Timoleague, Co. Cork, Ireland

Simon and Jude

October 28

Virtually nothing is known about the remaining apostles, except that Simon was described as "the Zealot," denoting a particularly devout Jew, or perhaps a particularly enthusiastic follower of Christ, and that Jude, considered the patron saint of hopeless causes, was also called Thaddaeus. He was referred to as "not Iscariot," to distinguish him from the disciple who betrayed Christ. Tradition has equated him with Jude, the brother of our Lord, writer of the Epistle, but this is extremely doubtful.

This jewellike Crucifixion and Last Supper window, one of artist Evie Hone's late works, is her most famous commission. As she depicts the apostles, it is ironically Judas Iscariot who stands out, sitting at the front, his hand in the bowl, with a darkened face. The fact that it is difficult to identify the other apostles individually serves to remind us Christ called not the great but the ordinary. As we have seen, Peter and John were dominant figures and while the characters of some of the others emerge clearly from the gospel accounts, the remainder are simply "disciples." All twelve were present at the Last Supper and all but Judas Iscariot saw the risen Christ and witnessed his Ascension. It was the remaining eleven, some rather anonymous, who received Christ's commission to "go and make disciples of all nations, baptizing them in the name of the Father and of the Son and of the Holy Spirit, and teaching them to obey everything that I have commanded you." (Matt. 28:19-20)

The Last Supper, *Evie Hone, 1949-52, Eton College Chapel, Windsor, Berkshire, England*

Mary and Martha

July 29

MARY AND HER sister, Martha, reacted differently when they welcomed Jesus to their home in Bethany. Martha, "distracted by her many tasks," complained her sister had left all the work to her. Jesus gently replied, "Martha, Martha, you are worried and distracted by many things; … Mary has chosen the best part." (Luke 10:40-42) In this window, Martha, the hassled cook in a full house, gestures in despair at Mary, who watches Jesus intently, oblivious of any domestic needs. Martha became the patron saint of housewives, representing the faithful love with which countless women have exercised ministry in the daily round of washing, cleaning, and cooking. Mary, however, is the prototype of women's public ministry. That she "sat at the Lord's feet" signifies she was a disciple, charged with the same mission as the twelve. Women's public ministry continued in the young church, as exemplified by Phoebe, "a deacon," and Prisc[ill]a, a fellow worker with Paul in Rome. (Rom. 16: 1-3)

When their brother Lazarus died, Mary and Martha were convinced Jesus would have healed Lazarus had he been there in time. Martha's belief that "even now … God will give you whatever you ask of him," prompts Jesus to say: "I am the resurrection and the life," and Martha replies, "Yes, Lord, I believe that you are the Messiah." (John 11:1-44) Yet the fragility of human faith is shown by her amazement when Jesus raises Lazarus.

Christ in the House of Mary and Martha, *Abraham van Linge, 1641,*
University College Chapel, Oxford, England

Joseph of Arimathea

March 17

JOSEPH OF ARIMATHEA is principally remembered for his compassion in giving the body of the crucified Christ an honorable burial. In Jewish society, crucifixion, being reserved for the lowest of the low—foreigners and slaves—implied utter contempt, yet Joseph, a respectable Jew, risked his reputation by asking Pilate for Christ's body and burying it in a new tomb, possibly the one he had reserved for himself.

This roundel may be too high for visitors to make out the detail, but the pathos is apparent even in the outlines. While Joseph supports Christ's lifeless body, Mary holds his drooping hands and Nicodemus kneels to remove the nails from his feet. John, grief stricken, can hardly bear to look. The extent of Joseph's daring is hinted at by the conical cap which he wears, for he was a member of the Jewish Council. (His assistant, Nicodemus, as a Pharisee, is also given a cap.)

Joseph was not a conventional hero, however. John implies he was a timid man, "a disciple of Jesus, but a secret one because of his fear of the Jews." (John 19:38) Luke describes him as "a good and righteous man, ... waiting expectantly for the kingdom of God." (Luke 23:50-51) Perhaps he was just a careful, thoughtful man, reluctant to disturb the *status quo*; whatever the case, when it really counted, he did what he knew to be right.

The Deposition, *twelfth century, Chartres Cathedral, France*

The Women at the Tomb

THE WOMEN AT the tomb are commonly called "the three Marys." Certainly, they were three of the many women who followed Christ and one of them was Mary Magdalene (overleaf), but the identity of the others is uncertain, so we commemorate them not so much as individuals but as exemplars. Similarly, those who have ministered to the dead of war, famine, and fever are mostly nameless to us but are known to God.

After the Crucifixion, these women followed Joseph of Arimathea and saw where he buried Christ. At dawn on the first day of the week, having observed the Sabbath, they returned with spices and ointments to anoint his body. Finding the stone rolled away from the tomb, they went in and saw it was empty. This is the moment captured in this sombre depiction. Mary Magdalene's body language tells all. Sinking to her knees, she stares in disbelief at the empty tomb. The downward turn of her mouth spells dismay. Her confusion is suggested by her hands—is she stretching them toward the tomb or lifting them to her head in dismay?

All three are desolate, for they have not yet seen the angel who appears beside them and asks, "Why do you look for the living among the dead? He is not here but has risen." (Luke 23:55-24:5)

The Women at the Tomb, *Lavers & Barraud, m.1875,*
Church of St. Lawrence, Mereworth, Kent, England

Mary Magdalene

July 22

Although Mary of Magdala is often identified both with Mary of Bethany *and* the repentant, unnamed woman who bathed Christ's feet with her tears and dried them with her hair, all we know about her is that she was healed by Christ, became a disciple, was present at the Crucifixion, and was the first person to whom he appeared after the Resurrection. This alone lends her great prominence, for it might have been expected he would appear to some of the apostles, but he *also* entrusted her with the task of telling them the good news.

On the first Easter morning, Mary went to the tomb and found it empty. Turning away, puzzled and tearful, she met a man whom she mistook as a gardener and asked if he had moved the body. John's account is stripped of all but the riveting dialogue: "Jesus said to her, 'Mary!' she turned and said to him in Hebrew, 'Rabboni!' (which means Teacher)." (John 20:16)

This sixteenth-century Flemish panel shows the extent to which glass may be influenced by time and place. The detail—the farmyard with neat picket fence, Christ's rustic garb, and wide-brimmed hat, Mary's coiffure and jewelry—makes it a very interesting depiction, but Mary isn't looking at Christ, nor he at her, and there is no air of excitement, so the intense drama of the moment is lost.

The Risen Christ Appears to Mary Magdalene, *sixteenth century,*
Llanwenllwyfo Church, Anglesey, Wales

Mark

April 25

THE WRITER OF the second gospel is usually identified with the John Mark mentioned in Acts. If so, he was the son of a believer called Mary, and a cousin of Barnabas (p. 69). Their home in Jerusalem was a meeting place for the early church and many had gathered there to pray when Peter was imprisoned. It is probable the whole household was Christian for, on the night of his miraculous release, when Peter appeared at the gate, the maid was "so overjoyed" she left him standing at the gate while she told everyone the good news. (Acts 12:12-18) Mark is not mentioned in the story, but was almost certainly there.

It is thought Mark may have been the young man mentioned in Mark 14 as following Christ after his arrest, wearing only a linen cloth. When some of the crowd caught hold of him, he left the cloth and ran away naked!

Mark's role in the early church is documented in Acts of the Apostles. He accompanied Paul and Barnabas on their first missionary journey, but deserted them and returned to Jerusalem. Paul, therefore, refused to take him on his second journey and this caused a rift with Barnabas, who took Mark with him to Cyprus. This gave him a chance to reestablish himself among the early missionaries, and, in time, he and Paul were reconciled. It is probable that he was with Paul in Rome.

Mark, *William Burges, Saunders & Co., 1868, Holy Trinity Church, Crosshaven, Co. Cork, Ireland*

Luke

October 18

THERE IS NO doubt the person who wrote Luke's Gospel also wrote the Acts of the Apostles, the single greatest record of the young church. Acts alone gives us accounts of Pentecost and Peter's subsequent spectacular development, the early persecutions, Paul's conversion, and all the early missionary endeavors.

It is not proven, but probable, that he is the same as the Luke who was one of Paul's fellow workers in the very early days of the church. One of the most appealing aspects of Acts is that Luke sometimes changes the narrative from "they" to "we." Thus, when Paul had a vision leading him to make his first expedition into Europe, Luke writes, "We set sail from Troas" and gives a vivid account of their reception in Philippi. (Acts 16:11 ff.) In fact, his itinerary is so detailed it suggests that Luke kept a diary as they traveled. He accompanied Paul to Rome and writes an invaluable description of the journey, with the same sensitive approach found in Luke's Gospel. Thus his riveting report of the storm and shipwreck ends with their safe landing on Malta and the comment: "The natives showed us unusual kindness." (Acts 27:13- 28:2)

Luke's role as the patron saint of medicine is based on Paul's reference to him as "the beloved physician" (Col. 4:14), but a doctor's insight would also explain his Gospel's empathy with the suffering.

Luke, *Lavers, Barraud & Westlake, 1879, Church of St. Vincent, Littlebourne, Kent, England*

Matthias

May 14

ONE OF THE first things the believers did after Pentecost was to appoint a new apostle to replace Judas Iscariot. It was Peter, as leader of the apostles, who guided them to choose one of the men who had been with them throughout Christ's earthly ministry and had shared their Resurrection experience. Two names were proposed—Justus and Matthias—and they all prayed for guidance. Then they cast lots (in faith that God would direct the outcome), the lot fell on Matthias and he was enrolled as an apostle. (Acts 1:15-26) It is this ceremony which is illustrated in H. W. Lonsdale's vignette (right). Matthias kneels prayerfully and humbly before Peter, who is asking God's blessing on the new apostle, while another of the apostles watches supportively.

Matthias, of course, was not ordained, nor had any of the other apostles been ordained or even baptized by Christ. There is not any suggestion the apostles subsequently elected anyone else to make up their number; when we speak of the apostolic succession, we refer to the continuity of ministry within the church. So, Matthias holds a unique position in the history of the church and yet he is not mentioned again in the New Testament, so we know nothing else about him. His very obscurity is a reminder of the saints whose goodness and service is known only to God.

Matthias, H. W. Lonsdale, c.1890s (restored and reordered in 1993 by Meg Lawrence),
Church of St. Matthias, Stocksbridge, Yorkshire, England

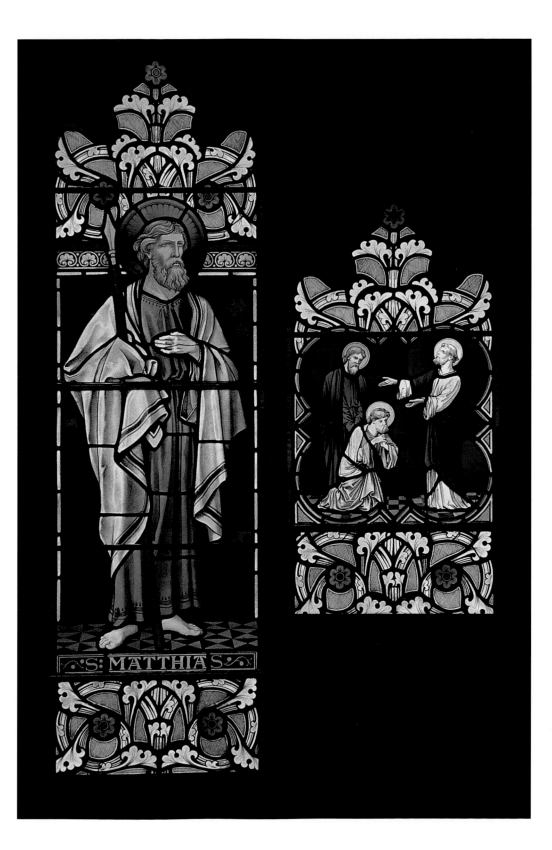

S: MATTHIAS

Stephen

December 26

ALTHOUGH JAMES THE Great was the first *apostle* to die for his faith, Stephen is the first Christian martyr. Stephen was one of the seven deacons chosen to safeguard the interests of the Greek-speaking Christians in Jerusalem.

Stephen, "full of grace and power, did great wonders and signs among the people" but his teaching so challenged the cherished beliefs of some of the Jews they accused him of blasphemy. During his speech to the Jewish Council, "his face was like the face of an angel" but "they became enraged and ground their teeth." The final straw came when Stephen gazed upwards and said, "I see the heavens opened and the Son of Man standing at the right hand of God!" Not waiting for a verdict, they dragged him out of the city and stoned him.

Stephen's dying words, echoing those of the crucified Christ, have provided inspiration for martyrs through the centuries. As he was pelted with stones, he prayed, "Lord Jesus, receive my spirit." Then he cried, "Lord, do not hold this sin against them," and died. (Acts 7:8-60)

Stephen's death proved to be a watershed for the church, as it heralded widespread persecution in Jerusalem and caused the Christians to disperse, taking the gospel to other cities and towns. This was an enormous step toward the spread of the Christian church.

The Stoning of Stephen, *Hardman & Co., c.1875, Norwich Cathedral, England*

Paul

THE DAMASCUS ROAD

January 25/June 29

THE CALL OF Paul is unlike that of Matthew, for Paul was extremely respectable. Known as Saul until after his conversion, he was a strict Pharisee, who considered it his duty to purge Judaism of this Christian "blasphemy." (He is shown on page 60 holding the coats of the stone-throwers at the martyrdom of Stephen.)

The window opposite highlights the drama of Paul's experience. "Still breathing threats and murder against the disciples," he was on his way to Damascus, when "suddenly a light from heaven flashed around him. He fell to the ground and heard a voice saying to him, 'Saul, Saul, why do you persecute me?' He asked, 'Who are you, Lord?' The reply came, 'I am Jesus, whom you are persecuting.'" (Acts 9:3-5) Paul was immediately won over to Christ and, although he had lost his sight, went on to Damascus to receive instructions. In that city God revealed to a disciple named Ananias he was to baptize Saul, because he was to be the apostle of the Gentiles. Putting aside his fear, he greeted Saul, who immediately regained his sight and received the Holy Spirit. From that moment he became a formidable preacher of the gospel, for the very qualities which made Paul so feared a persecutor of the church, made him an outstanding apostle.

Paul on the Damascus Road, *Hardman & Co., c.1875, Norwich Cathedral, England*

Paul

AT THE AREOPAGUS

A S APOSTLE TO the Gentiles, Paul undertook two major missionary journeys. In some places great numbers came to faith, but in others he was imprisoned or attacked. In Athens Paul was quickly drawn into debate with the philosophers. Even under Roman rule, Athens remained the intellectual center of the ancient world, so there was immediate interest in a teacher of a new religion. Paul, invited to speak at the Areopagus, shrewdly adapted his message to the local situation, beginning with the Greek concept of God as creator of and presence within the universe.

In the center of William Morris's window Paul stands on the steps of the Areopagus in full flow. His argument proceeds to the human search for God, pointing out that he is not far from us, "for," as the text below the window reads, "in him we live and move and have our being." (Acts17:28) Paul's argument thus far was persuasive but most of his audience ridiculed his teaching on the Resurrection and he won few converts in Athens. Morris suggests this mixed reaction by drawing some people who are patently not paying attention: one has turned his back and others look bored. This scheme of windows for Selsley was the first commission undertaken by the firm of Morris and Company.

Paul at the Areopagus, *William Morris, Morris & Co., 1861-2, All Saints' Church, Selsley, Gloucestershire, England*

Paul

A P R I S O N E R O F C H R I S T J E S U S

S UCH WAS THE hatred Paul aroused among the Jewish establishment in Jerusalem that in about A.D. 60 the Roman authorities had to rescue him from a mob which would have killed him. After two years' imprisonment in Caesarea, he appealed to Caesar and was sent to Rome. Nothing definite is known about the subsequent events which led to his martyrdom in about A.D. 65.

Paul wrote several powerful letters from prison, in which he styled himself as a prisoner *of* and prisoner *for* Christ. "I regard everything as loss," he wrote, "because of the surpassing value of knowing Christ Jesus my Lord. For his sake I have suffered the loss of all things, and I regard them as rubbish, in order that I may gain Christ and be found in him." (Phil. 3:8-9) Texts such as this have sustained many a martyr of a later age.

Rowan LeCompte's depiction of Paul in chains reminds us of another great Pauline text, "May I never boast of anything except the cross of our Lord Jesus Christ, by which the world has been crucified to me and I to the world." (Gal. 6:14) Paul's gaze is fixed on the *empty* cross, for it is Christ risen, ascended, and glorified who is his Lord.

Paul, a Prisoner of Christ Jesus, *Rowan LeCompte, 1984, Washington National Cathedral*

Barnabas

June 11

ONE OF THE early leaders of the church in Jerusalem, Barnabas is given the title "apostle," although not one of the original twelve. He obviously had a way with people and is remembered for a great ministry of encouragement. Sent to encourage the new believers in Antioch, "he exhorted them all to remain faithful to the Lord … and a great many people were brought to the Lord." (Acts 11:23-4)

Appropriately, this window shows Barnabas with Paul, for he played an important part in Paul's ministry. It was he who persuaded the church in Jerusalem to accept Paul as a disciple, who brought him as an assistant to Antioch, he who accompanied Paul on the first missionary journey. In fact, Barnabas was seen as the senior partner at that stage but was later overshadowed by his protégé. The window shows them at Lystra, in Turkey. Much to their horror, their ministry there led the people to acclaim them as gods but human fickleness was soon demonstrated when the people turned against them. In the window you can see men with furious faces, about to hurl stones at the pair.

Barnabas continued to work with Paul, and on his own, as in Cyprus, where he is considered the founder of the church. There is no greater accolade than the one given to him by Luke: "a good man, full of the Holy Spirit and of faith." (Acts 11:24)

Barnabas and Paul Stoned at Lystra, *1535-47, King's College Chapel, Cambridge, England*

Timothy

January 26

TIMOTHY WAS ONE of Paul's fellow workers. The son of a Greek gentile father and a Jewish Christian woman, he lived in Lystra and it was there Paul recruited him as a colleague on his second missionary journey. (The predella opposite shows him as a child, with his mother.) He traveled with Paul and Silas through Turkey and onto Greece. This must have been a marvelous apprenticeship for the youthful Timothy, for whom Paul developed a deep affection. From an early stage, Paul entrusted difficult commissions to him, leaving him to look after the Christians in Beroea and Thessalonica with Silas and sending him to deal with trouble in various churches. Paul wrote to the Philippians of his hope of sending Timothy, adding, "I have no one like him who will be genuinely concerned for your welfare … Timothy's worth you know, how like a son with a father he has served with me in the work of the gospel." (Phil. 2:20-22)

Paul later sent him to Ephesus, of whose church he was the first leader. The pastoral epistles, 1 and 2 Timothy, were sent to encourage him in his work there. He is always depicted as a young man and is included in this window, along with a youthful Samuel, David, and John the Evangelist, to commemorate an Oxford undergraduate who died tragically.

Timothy, *Edward Burne-Jones, Morris & Co., 1871, Christ Church Cathedral, Oxford, England*

DABIT
TIBI
DOMI
NUS IN

DMN
IBUS
INTEL
LECTU

timotheus episcopus

THE CROWN OF LIFE

Clement

November 23

A S FAR AS CAN be established, Peter was succeeded as leader of the church at Rome first by Cletus, then by Clement. The apostles had no ecclesiastical structures but traveled around preaching, baptizing, and presiding at the Eucharist, appointing new ministers by the laying on of hands. The formalized division into bishops, priests, and deacons came gradually, in response to the organizational needs of the rapidly expanding church. Likewise, the first bishops did not have the monarchical power of their medieval successors, so Clement (who may be the Clement referred to by Paul in Philippians 4) was in fact "bishop" of Rome but not "pope" as we understand it. Clement's *Letter to the church at Corinth* assumed scriptural importance in the early church for its pastoral leadership.

This two-in-one cameo, a section of window depicting Clement's life from baptism to martyrdom (c.100), reflects medieval teaching on the apostolic succession and the primacy of the pope. On one side, Clement is being baptized in a wooden tub by Peter; on the other, Clement is standing at the altar celebrating the Eucharist. Clement, as bishop, is made to look exactly like Peter to stress the unbroken succession in the see of Rome. Back to back, they are administering the two great sacraments of the church, as a reminder of the continuity of worship from the first days of the apostles.

Clement, 1225-30, Church of St. Kunibert, Cologne, Germany

Ignatius and Polycarp

October 17 and February 23

THE SECOND-CENTURY church, believing Ignatius and Polycarp had known Peter, John, or Paul, regarded them as a precious link to the apostles. As early bishops, they certainly occupy a vital position in the expanding the church.

Ignatius, also called Theophorus (God-bearer), was the second or third Bishop of Antioch. About A.D. 110, he was sentenced to death and taken to Rome, where he was thrown to wild beasts. On the way to Rome, he met the young bishop, Polycarp, at Smyrna and wrote four letters of encouragement and guidance to various Christian communities. Later on the journey, he wrote three more letters, including one to Polycarp. These letters afford an invaluable picture of the contemporary church and reveal a gentle bishop, who was very ready to die for the faith. Polycarp's teaching that the unity of the church lies in Christ alone ("Where Jesus Christ is, there is the catholic church"), is still important in modern ecumenical dialogue.

Polycarp's long episcopacy ended with his martyrdom about 155. The account of his death, written by the church at Symrna, is the earliest authentic record of a martyrdom apart from that of Stephen. Asked by the proconsul to swear by the emperor's guardian spirit and to deny Christ, he responded stoutly that he had served his Lord for eighty-six years and would not now desert him. Polycarp then offered a prayer and was burned alive.

Ignatius and Polycarp, Hardman & Co., early 1870s,
All Saints' Church, Cheltenham, Gloucestershire, England

TO · THE · GLORY · OF · GOD
HENRY · JOHN · STOKES · WHO

AND · IN · LOVING · MEMORY · OF
DIED · APRIL · 29 · 1872 · AGED · 29

helena

August 18

ELENA IS FAMOUS as the mother of Constantine, the first emperor to grant toleration to the Christian church. Born about 255, she married the emperor, Constantius Chlorus. We do not know when she became a Christian. Nor is it clear how influential she was in bringing about her son's conversion.

Persecution of Christianity had continued into the fourth century, yet almost half the population of the empire was Christian. Constantine's father had been fairly tolerant but it was a major watershed when, in 313, Constantine extended freedom of worship and returned confiscated churches to the Christian community. While Constantine was a far-from-saintly convert, Helena felt free to devote the rest of her life to the spread of the gospel. She spent much time in the Holy Land, where she was renowned for her concern for the poor. She was also instrumental in establishing churches on hallowed sites.

In art, Helena is often shown holding part of the cross, because she is associated about that time with the discovery of the cross, buried at Calvary. Sometimes she bears the weight of a large section, but in this panel the piece of wood looks more like a wand, for all the emphasis is on Helena's imperial status. The formal decoration, restrained coloring, the gold crown, rich robes, fine features, and stylish coiffure, combine to present an image of a dignified empress. She died in old age about A.D. 330.

Helena, *1345, Regensburg Cathedral, Germany*

Athanasius and Basil

May 2 and January 1, 2

THANASIUS AND BASIL here represent the fourth-century theologians of the Eastern church. With John Chrysostom and Gregory of Nazianzus they are known as "the Greek doctors of the church," while Basil was also one of "the Cappadocian fathers," along with Gregory of Nazianzus and Gregory of Nyssa.

Athanasius was born in Alexandria about 296. As a deacon, he accompanied his bishop to the first council of Nicea in 325, at which Arianism was condemned. As Bishop of Alexandria from 328 until his death about 373, he made a major contribution to the defeat of the Arian heresy which denied Christ's divinity. In his writings he pointed out clearly that if Christ was not God, Christianity was baseless and Christians committed idolatry in worshiping him. Athanasius did not compose the creed which is called after him, but he did write the important *Life of Antony* and biblical commentaries, some of which have survived.

Basil continued the fight against Arianism and followed Athanasius's lead in developing the Eastern church's theology of the Trinity. Born in Caesarea about 330, he was a member of a very distinguished Christian family. His parents, grandmother, elder sister, and two younger brothers (one of them was Gregory of Nyssa) all achieved sainthood. Bishop of Caesarea from 370 until his death in 379, many of his writings are extant and remain an important historical and theological source.

Athanasius and Basil, *Hardman & Co., early 1870s, All Saints' Church, Cheltenham, Gloucestershire, England*

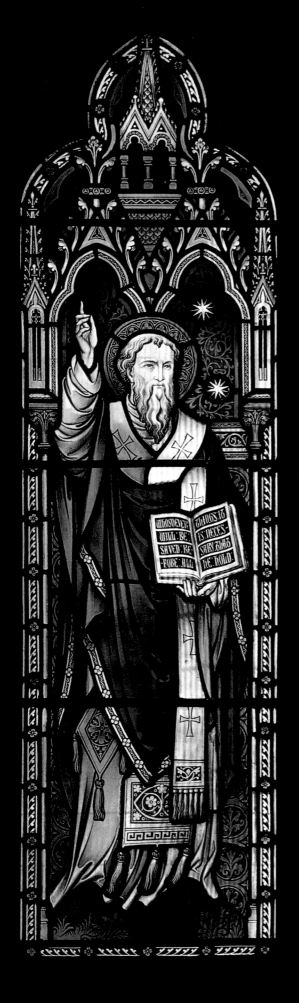
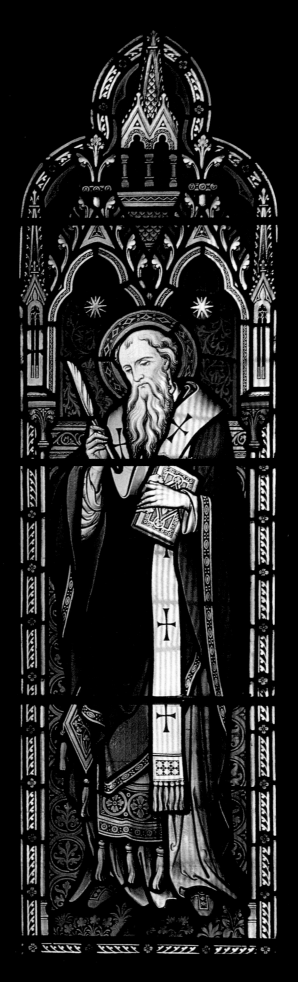

Denis

October 9

ENIS OR DIONYSIUS of Paris was a third-century bishop, believed to have been martyred about 258. Long celebrated as the patron saint of France, very little is actually known about him. By the sixth century, however, he was portrayed as a missionary sent to France in 250 and subsequently beheaded along with Rusticus, a priest, and Eleutherius, a deacon, in Paris, at the place now known as 'Montmartre' (Martyrs' Hill).

The sparse historical facts are less familiar than the later legends: thus Denis, the third-century martyr, became confused with one of St. Paul's converts at Athens, Dionysius the Areopagite. Additional confusion arose with the attribution to *him* of the writings of a fifth-century ecclesiastical writer known as the Pseudo-Dionysius.

This window depicts Denis as a "head-carrier" (*cephalophore*), one of a number of martyrs believed to have carried their severed heads to their burial place, in this instance the abbey church of St. Denis in Paris.

A remarkably lively Denis is accompanied by angels, one of whom is pointing the way, while another is gently guiding him forward. Their demeanor and the vibrancy of coloring focuses attention not on the horror of beheading, but on the power of God, echoing Paul's words, "we are afflicted in every way, but not crushed; perplexed, but not driven to despair; persecuted, but not forsaken; struck down but not destroyed." (2 Cor. 4: 8-9)

Denis, thirteenth century, Lincoln Cathedral, England

Martin of Tours

November 11

ARTIN WAS UNUSUAL among the early saints, in that he did not suffer martyrdom but was honored as the father of monasticism in France. Born in Hungary c.316, he was a young officer in the Roman army at Amiens when an act of kindness changed his life.

This roundel in the Chapel of St. Martin in Canterbury Cathedral, in England, shows Martin astride his horse, cutting his cloak in half with his sword to share it with a half-naked beggar. Recognizing Christ in that poor man, he realized the truth of Christ's saying, "Just as you did [an act of mercy] to one of the least of these who are members of my family, you did it to me." (Matt. 25:40) He was baptized and soon came to feel that "as Christ's soldier," he could not fight, so asked to leave the army.

After obtaining his discharge, he became a hermit, and in 360 founded the first monastery in France. This was a semiremetical community and, even after he became Bishop of Tours in 370, Martin still lived as a solitary at Marmontier. That too developed into a monastery and his example led to the foundation of many other monasteries. Venerated throughout Christendom, his influence extended to the farthest reaches of Scotland and to North Africa in the centuries after his death in 397.

Martin of Tours, *thirteenth century, Canterbury Cathedral, England*

George

April 23

THE LEGEND OF George slaying the dragon is very famous. This window typifies the image of a young man in armor, slaying a fiercesome beast with his sword, but there is no proof of the tradition. Even in the sixth century, when George was widely venerated as a soldier saint, it was acknowledged God alone knew the historical facts. A martyr of the third or fourth century, George was probably killed in Palestine; the dragon story (like that of Patrick casting out all the snakes from Ireland) may say more about his conquest of evil than his military prowess.

Nevertheless, George's reputation as the patron saint and model of soldiers became very strong in the East and spread to the West through the Crusaders. The patron saint of many countries, nowhere was he assimilated more into the national culture than in England. Even today his symbol of a red cross on a white background is the English element of the national flag and the George Cross remains one of the highest awards for bravery. After the two World Wars many memorial windows to fallen soldiers took the theme of St. George, equating him with the "Faithful Warrior." This fifteenth-century German glass makes a similar point in the soldier's statue "carved" in the architectural canopy. Thus George represented all those who gave their lives in defense of their country.

George, 1483, Hesse Museum, Darmstadt (formerly in Neckarsteinach), Germany

Cecilia

November 22

TWO SAINTS ARE included in this book of whom hardly anything is known, to demonstrate the power of their cult. The only ascertainable facts about Cecilia are that she founded a church in Rome and was buried in a place of honor. She probably lived in the second or third century.

By the sixth century, Cecilia was venerated as a virgin martyr. The story went that on her wedding day she told her fiancé, Valerian, of her vocation to virginity and won him over to the Christian faith and that she later suffered a terrible martyr's death. None of this is reliable, however, for it is derived from a Passion of St. Cecily, which was possibly about *another* Cecily who had been martyred, and which may be a largely mythical construction.

It is not difficult to see why Cecilia's cult grew. In casting her as a virgin, she represented the innumerable women who devoted their lives to God and refused to marry. That she later became the patron of musicians probably derived from the Passion account of her singing "in her heart" to God, while musicians played for her wedding.

Edward Burne-Jones, chief designer of William Morris and Company, the English Arts and Crafts firm, was one of the outstanding stained-glass artists of the nineteenth century. His Cecilia is innocent, virginal, and focused, as she plays the organ which is her symbol.

Cecilia, *Edward Burne-Jones, Morris & Co., 1875, Christ Church Cathedral, Oxford, England*

Nicholas

December 6

ALL WE KNOW for certain about Nicholas is that he was a fourth-century bishop of Myra in Turkey, yet he became one of the most popular of the medieval saints. Much better known is the figure derived from him, "Santa Claus!" A vast body of legend surrounded Nicholas, in the best known of which he restored to life three children who had been pickled in brine. For this reason he became the patron saint of children, but he also had a particular association with sailors and merchants. His cult was so strong that countless churches were dedicated to him and he became the patron of many countries, including Russia.

This lovely illustration of a legendary posthumous miracle is high in the nave clerestory in York Minster. A man is brought to court by a Jew for nonpayment of a debt. On his way to the dock he hands his staff to the Jew and then swears he has returned the money. The man is acquitted, takes back his staff from the Jew and leaves. On the way home the man is knocked down and killed by a horse and cart. (The horseman stands against a brilliant blue background, while the culprit lies under the cartwheel.) The disputed money is found inside his broken staff. The Jew asks Nicholas to restore the man to life and this miracle leads him to become a Christian.

Nicholas, *twelfth century, York Minster, England*

Catherine

formerly November 25

THE ENTRY FOR Catherine in several books of the saints reads "cult suppressed in 1969." While some of the early saints are very shadowy figures, so little is known about Catherine of Alexandria she is no longer officially recognized as a saint. Far from being (as was long believed) a virgin martyr in imperial Egypt, it is now thought she may be merely a pious invention. There are, however, many churches dedicated to her, for she was for centuries a popular cult figure in both the East and West.

The basic story is of a highly intelligent aristocrat, skillfully dismissing the arguments of pagan philosophers. When, as a Christian, she refused to marry the emperor, he threw her in prison and tried to break her determination on a spiked wheel. The wheel shattered and Catherine was finally beheaded, but angels took her body to Mount Sinai, where an Orthodox monastery was built to honor her.

The resplendent portrayal captures the aristocratic lady superbly, albeit in the opulent costume of quite another period. Unlike the glum philosopher behind her, Catherine is serene and in control, as is evidenced not just by her tranquil expression but the poise with which she holds the instrument of her death and by placing a tiny, useless wheel at her feet. With the decorative detail, especially on Catherine's ruby gown, it is a splendid example of Peter Hemmel von Andlau's artistry and technical brilliance.

Catherine, *Peter Hemmel von Andlau, c.1480, Hesse Museum, Darmstadt, Germany*
(probably from Kloster Nonnberg, Salzburg, Austria)

Jerome

September 30

AMBROSE AND AUGUSTINE, with Jerome and Gregory, are known as the Latin doctors of the church. Of the four, the greatest scholar was Jerome. Born in Dalmatia about 341, he was brought up as a Christian and studied in Rome. Having spent some time as a hermit in Palestine, he later returned to Rome, where he was Pope Damasus's secretary. Although an ordained priest, Jerome knew his gift was not for pastoral ministry but for biblical interpretation. Determined to serve God as best he could, he eventually returned to Palestine to devote himself to prayer and study. He died in Bethlehem in 420.

His biblical commentaries established his reputation and remained standard reference works for many centuries. However, his fame was increased by his "Vulgate" translation of the Bible, commissioned by Pope Damasus and completed about the year 405. It would be difficult to overemphasize the importance to the church of this authoritative Latin translation of the Greek and Hebrew scriptures.

This roundel highlights Jerome's asceticism. Alone in a deserted spot, he has stripped off his robes and is kneeling in penitent prayer before a crucifix, which he has hung on a tree. The stone in his right hand is a weapon with which to beat his breast, in sorrow for his sins. However, the open book beside him is a reminder of his achievements as a writer.

Jerome, *seventeenth century, Church of St. Peter, Nowton, Norfolk, England*

Ambrose and Augustine

December 7 and August 28

A S NO SUITABLE window was found to illustrate Ambrose and Augustine together, Ambrose represents his protégé in a depiction by Pugin, father of the English nineteenth-century Gothic revival. The lawyer son of a Roman official, Ambrose was appointed governor of the province centered on Milan in about 370. He must have been impressive, for in 374 he was chosen by the people to be Bishop of Milan, despite the fact he was a recent convert, not yet baptized, let alone ordained. Yet, he became an eminent bishop, who tackled effectively the challenges of Arianism, paganism, and imperial tyranny. His reproof of Theodosius I for savage suppression of civil disorder showed him to be fearless in defending the gospel. The beehive at the base of his portrait denotes his "honeyed" eloquence, because he was also famed for his preaching and teaching. He died in 386.

Augustine represents the African church, because he came from Algeria. Born in 354, his mother, Monica, brought him up in the Christian faith but he was more interested in philosophy and rhetoric until, in Milan, he came under Ambrose's influence. After his baptism in 387, he returned to Africa and entered the religious life. As Bishop of Hippo from 396 until his death in 430, he applied his considerable intellect to theology. Of his many extant works, his *Confessions* and *The City of God* are Christian classics. We can all identify with Augustine's inner struggle between worldly fulfilment and holiness, encapsulated in his saying, "Make me chaste, Lord, but not yet."

Ambrose, A. W. N. Pugin, Hardman & Co., c.1850, Church of St. Paul, Brighton, England

✛

Gregory the Great

September 3

GREGORY I, OR "Gregory the Great" was one of the most influential of all the popes. This portrayal of him is typical in so far as he is vested as pope and carrying a double-barred cross, but he is often shown reading or writing, a tribute to the significance of his writings. Born into an aristocratic Roman family about 540, Gregory disposed of his property and used the proceeds to found monasteries, became a monk, and was pope from 590 until his death in 604.

Europe had not begun to recover from the disastrous effects of the collapse of the Roman Empire, which had brought dislocation to church and society alike. In a time of political instability, Gregory steered the church with far-seeing inspiration, centralizing its administration and establishing its independence of secular authority. He also developed a new concept of the papacy, typified by calling himself as pope, "the servant of the servants of God." He is also remembered as the pope who sent Augustine to Canterbury in England.

His *Liber Regulae Pastoralis* became the pastoral guide for bishops throughout the church, while his writings on the saints in the *Dialogues* became enormously popular. For centuries Gregory stood for all that was best in church government and his letters and sermons were extremely influential. Gregorian plainsong chant is a lasting memorial to Gregory the liturgist.

Gregory, fourteenth century, All Saints' Church, Langport, Somerset, England

Patrick

March 17

PATRICK, THE NATIONAL saint of Ireland, is revered in all the countries to which the Irish have emigrated. Scholars disagree about his birth date: some argue for about 390, others for about 410. Likewise, there is not a consensus for the date of his death, but we do know that he was born into a Christian family in Roman Britain, from where, at the age of sixteen, he was carried off as a slave to Ireland.

After six years, Patrick escaped but returned some years later as a bishop, probably to a Christian community in the northeast. He was by no means the first evangelist of the Irish, but he traveled widely to bring the gospel to those who had not heard it, causing in the process opposition from his fellow bishops in Britain.

Patrick wrote his *Confession* to testify to God's transforming love in his life and to justify his ministry in Ireland. It and his *Letter to the soldiers of Coroticus*, the Scottish warlord who had kidnapped and killed some of Patrick's new converts, are the first extant writings of any Christian of the Irish or British church.

This picture of Patrick as a simply dressed shepherd of his people captures the essence of the saint who wrote of Coroticus's raid: "Fierce wolves have swallowed up the Lord's flock," and who called himself "the least of all the faithful" and "the slave of Christ."

Patrick, *Catherine O'Brien, 1925, Church of St. Bartholomew, Dublin, Ireland*

To the Glory
of GOD.

and in loving
memory of
FRANCES
LOUISA
CONNER

1925

Benedict

July 11

ORN IN ITALY about 480, Benedict was a hermit whose sanctity attracted so many disciples he had to organize them in communities. About 530 he founded a large monastery at Monte Cassino, which he led until his death, about 547. The biographical details are insignificant compared with the "Holy Rule" which he drew up for his communities. This practical guide to living the gospel has a universal appeal, which speaks to people today as they try to follow Christ.

As Benedict points out, "This rule is not meant to be a burden for you. It should help you discover … how great is the freedom to which you are called." It is freedom to find fulfilment in praying, working and loving, as "the Lord in his love shows us the way of life." Benedict teaches that, if we look for God in all things, work springs from prayer, as prayer from work and both are inspired by love.

In the following centuries the Benedictines became so influential in the Western church they shaped its development until the Reformation. In England half of the cathedrals, including Norwich, lived under the Benedictine rule. Benedict is the central figure in the left light of this large window, which commemorates several other leading Benedictine saints and monks, including the scholars Bede and Anselm, and bishops Oswald of Worcester and Ethelwold of Winchester, all in their characteristic black.

Benedict and the Benedictines, *Moira Forsyth, 1964, Norwich Cathedral, England*

Aidan and Hilda

August 31 and November 17

AIDAN, AN IRISH monk at the Columban monastery of Iona, was sent in 635 as a missionary to Northumbria at the request of the newly crowned king, Oswald. Having been consecrated bishop, he established his headquarters on Lindisfarne. Recognizing the need for English evangelists to work among their own people, he founded a monastery at Lindisfarne where, as abbot, he oversaw the training of local boys for ministry.

Aidan traveled on foot throughout his huge diocese, establishing new church communities and encouraging the faithful. Much of Aidan's success lay in the fact he so patently practiced what he preached. Despite his friendship with the king, there were not any trappings of power and his lifestyle was simple and ascetic. At Lindisfarne, likewise, he made it a priority to look after the poor. He died at Bamburgh, on the Northumbrian coast of England, in 651, already revered for his gentle goodness and strong leadership.

Hilda was born in Northumbria in 614, a great-niece of King Edwin. Aidan made her abbess at Hartlepool in 649, and she later founded a new monastery for women *and* men at Whitby. Her most significant contribution centers on the Synod of Whitby, which she called in 664 to decide between the Roman and Celtic liturgical and disciplinary customs. Her acceptance of the decision in favor of Roman customs proved a vital contribution to the peace and unity of the church in England. She died in 680.

Aidan and Hilda, *Christopher Whall, 1901, Gloucester Cathedral, England*

Cuthbert and Chad

March 20 / September 4 and March 2

CUTHBERT WAS BORN about 634, almost certainly in Northumbria, England. As a monk and later abbot-bishop of Lindisfarne (which, after the council of Whitby, became a Benedictine monastery), he followed Aidan's example of journeying far and wide to minister to Christian communities, and was a man of great compassion. At heart, however, he was a contemplative who drew strength from solitary periods on the tiny island of Farne, in the company of the seabirds, otters, and seals. He died there in 687, and was buried at Lindisfarne. Although he had been a bishop for only two years, people had been so impressed by his sanctity that a cult grew quickly and, when the Vikings invaded in the ninth century, his relics were lovingly protected. They finally reached Durham, where his shrine became the focal point of the eleventh-century Norman cathedral.

Chad was a pupil of Aidan's at Lindisfarne, who followed his brother, St. Cedd, as abbot of Lastingham in Yorkshire. Cedd, who had founded Lastingham, later became bishop of the East Saxons and Chad was, in turn, made bishop of York, but Theodore, Archbishop of Canterbury, ruled he had been irregularly consecrated. Chad readily acceded and returned to Lastingham. Theodore was so impressed by Chad's humility that he was soon made bishop of Mercia. He died in Lichfield in 672. In art he is often shown, as here, holding a church.

Cuthbert and Chad, *Christopher Whall, 1901, Gloucester Cathedral, England*

Leger

October 2

THE VIVID COLORING adds to the drama of this scene. Gruesome as this is, it is less horrific than some depictions of Leger's martyrdom, in which he is show holding his eyes (or tongue) on a plate. Leger, also known as Leodegar, was one of a long succession of church leaders put to death for political reasons. Born near Arras in France about 616, he became a Benedictine monk and was made bishop of Autun in 653.

His insistence on strict discipline within the church aroused some opposition, but it was his close connection to the court of St. Bathildis, the queen regent of France, and then of her son, Clotaire III, which brought him into conflict with Ebroin, the mayor of the palace. The tyrannical Ebroin became increasingly frustrated by Leger's opposition, and in 679 had him blinded, mutilated, and finally murdered.

It comes across forcefully his assailants are taking great pleasure in torturing him in this window. They are standing on Leger to pin him down and the figure on the left has a nasty leer on his face. He has grasped the saint's head with both hands and is forcibly turning it toward the instrument of torture. The other assailant looks almost mad with blood-lust. Leger, with his miter still on his head, only lifts a hand to ward off his attacker. Leger is one of many saints, including Anastasia, Dorothy, Lawrence, and Sebastian, in this large Martyrs' Window (p. 7) in Freiburg, Germany.

Leger, c.1280, Freiburg Cathedral, Germany

Boniface

June 5

BONIFACE SPEARHEADED THE eighth-century English effort to evangelize Germany and the Netherlands. Born about 675, probably at Crediton, in Devon, England, his original name was Winfrith but he is always known as "Boniface," a Latin name for "a doer of good." At an early age he became a Benedictine monk, with a particular gift for teaching and preaching. In his forties he went to Europe as a missionary, serving first in Holland, then in Germany. Progress was slow and he went to Rome three times to seek papal support.

On returning from one of his journeys, he found the people had lapsed into their former superstitious practices. This window depicts Boniface's legendary show of God's strength, when he felled a giant oak, sacred to the god Thor. The crowd watched anxiously, sure something terrible would happen to him, but were convinced he had preached the truth all along when the tree split in four, in the shape of the cross, and Boniface stood there completely unharmed.

Boniface eventually made a great success of his mission to Germany. In old age, he took on a new mission to Holland and was martyred there in 754. His surviving correspondence reveals the "apostle of Germany" as a lovable optimist, full of faith in God's power. This is suggested in Albert Birkle's window by showing Boniface holding a pastoral staff in his left hand but the cross in his right hand.

Boniface, *Albert Birkle, 1959, Washington National Cathedral*

Ðunstan

May 19

UNSTAN, THE GREAT monastic reformer and Archbishop of Canterbury from 959 to 988, is commemorated in two triforium windows in Canterbury Cathedral. Dramatic scenes from his early life in Glastonbury, where he was born about 909, and from his ministry feature along with some of the miracles attributed to him. While the section opposite is less exciting, it is highly significant for it shows his ordination. It serves as a reminder of the apostolic succession, by which Christ's great commission to the apostles has been passed from generation to generation and of the Archbishop of Canterbury's role as leader of and focus for unity in the world-wide Anglican communion.

It was at the instigation of Edmund I that Dunstan began (c.943) to revive monastic life at Glastonbury in England. English monasticism had never recovered from the devastation of the Anglo-Saxons, but then, with royal support and the cooperation of St. Ethelwold and St. Oswald of Worcester, Dunstan initiated the revival. Many famous abbeys were founded or reestablished, among them Malmesbury and Westminster, and Dunstan guided them to adopt the Benedictine rule, while adapting it to the requirements of the tenth century.

Dunstan was a wise statesman, greatly relied on by King Edgar. It is interesting that the liturgy which he used at Edgar's consecration as king of England in 973 still forms the basis of the coronation ceremonies of the British sovereign.

Dunstan, *late twelfth century, Canterbury Cathedral, England*

Thomas Becket

December 29

THOMAS BECKET, ARCHBISHOP of Canterbury, died a martyr in his own cathedral in 1170. His story epitomizes the church-state power struggles which bedeviled medieval society, because, like many churchmen, he was also deeply involved in politics. In fact, as Henry II's Chancellor of the Exchequer, he was primarily a statesman until his appointment as Archbishop of Canterbury in 1162. At that time he was only a deacon, so he was ordained as a priest on the day before his consecration as a bishop! Thomas proved a thorn in Henry's side, stubbornly defending church interests. Exiled to France, he returned in 1170 but was murdered within days by a party of four knights anxious to fulfil the king's wish to be rid of his troublesome archbishop.

In the later Middle Ages pilgrims flocked to the cathedral (as in Chaucer's *Canterbury Tales*) to venerate Thomas. Their approach to his shrine was framed by twelve windows reminding them of the events of his life, death, and subsequent miracles. Dramatic vignettes showing the assassins bursting in the great door and one of them manhandling a terrified monk are among the earliest and best examples of English medieval glass, but this portrayal of an earlier reconciliation between Henry and Thomas is a later reconstruction. None of the depictions of Thomas is in original glass, because, in the 1530s, Henry VIII had Thomas's shrine and all the images of him destroyed.

Thomas Becket, c.1220 (this is a modern reconstruction of the original),
Canterbury Cathedral, England

Bernard of Clairvaux

August 20

BERNARD WAS BORN near Dijon, France, in 1090, the son of a Burgundian noble. A devout young man, he persuaded four of his brothers and a large number of friends to join him when he became a monk in the new monastery at Citeaux in 1113. Before long he was sent to establish another house at Clairvaux. That foundation was so successful it became the mother house of sixty-eight Cistercian houses in many countries. For this reason Bernard is considered one of the founders of the Cistercian movement and the prime figure behind its reforming influence. Popes, bishops, and kings looked to him for guidance.

This window shows Bernard (at left) and his monks (in white Cistercian habits) singing the night office, a reminder that the demanding daily offices were the dominant feature of daily life for Bernard. Nothing was as important as worship and it was the springboard for all his other work, especially for his writing and teaching. This is affirmed by the presence of kneeling angels with scrolls in their hands. In the foreground stands a honey pot, a reference to Bernard's title as "the honey-sweet teacher." His writings, especially his treatise *On the Love of God* appeal to the modern reader more than most medieval writings because, as he said himself, he wrote "to reach people's hearts," rather than to demonstrate his learning.

Bernard, *early sixteenth century, Church of St. Mary, Shrewsbury, England, made for the Cistercian abbey of Altenberg, Germany*

em in nocturis   uigilijs urr dñi   entim   a bño Bernardo   buana dilrctione   rationibus et su
freedbant auro ·   ab argento noniti sã   anno   y . j . 9 . 8 celebrauit   more mã raut et   aplio ſe iudio

Francis of Assisi

October 4

FRANCIS IS PROBABLY the most loved of the medieval saints. Born at Assisi about 1181, he was the son of a wealthy merchant and enjoyed a youth of luxury and idle revelry. However, a vision of Christ calling him to "repair my falling house," led him to pledge his life to one of poverty and service of the needy. He established in 1210 the Friars Minor (better known as Franciscans), to wander throughout the country preaching a simple but demanding faith to rich and poor alike.

Attracted by Francis's integrity and his infectious joy in the Lord, thousands of young men joined the order and its work soon spread abroad. To "repair" the church, Francis turned his back on all its manifestations of power. His insistence that his friars renounce not only personal but even corporate property and refuse ecclesiastical preferment marked them out in a church suffering many abuses. In word and action, the gospel was preached in its direct simplicity and people found it compelling.

Francis died at Assisi in 1226 and the church there remains a major center of pilgrimage to this day. He is represented here preaching to the birds. This reflects Francis's love of all God's creation, expressed in his *Canticle of the Sun*, best known in the hymn version:

All creatures of our God and King,
Lift up your voice and with us sing Hallelujah!

Francis, *fourteenth century, Kloster Kirche, Königsfelden, near Zurich, Switzerland*

Clare

August 11

LIKE FRANCIS, CLARE was born (c.1194) into a rich family in Assisi. As a young girl, she came under the influence of Francis, dedicated her life to the service of God and entered a Benedictine convent. In 1212 Francis guided her to establish a new community at the church of San Damiano at Assisi, and she drew up a "way of life" which marked the Poor Clares out from other nuns of the time. Originally her family had opposed her vocation but her sister, Agnes, and their widowed mother later joined her, and Agnes (also recognized as a saint) founded several communities of the Poor Clares.

The subdued coloring of the roundel and the bareness of the setting convey the ascetic simplicity which Francis and Clare cultivated. The lack of any architectural decoration or adornment in her dress reminds us Clare obtained from the pope the "privilege of poverty," the freedom to live solely on alms. The rejection of all property, a timely contrast to the wealth of some orders at the time, enabled Clare and her sisters to concentrate on spiritual priorities. Clare led her expanding community for forty years until her death in 1253, tempering austerity with tenderness (she went around at night tucking in the bedclothes for the sleeping nuns), and maintaining a delicate balance between the life of contemplation and active mission.

Clare, sixteenth century, Church of St. John the Divine, Rownhams, Hampshire, England

Antony of Padua

June 13

I T IS APPROPRIATE that glass chosen for Antony of Padua shows him preaching, because he is remembered primarily as an outstanding preacher. His extant sermons reveal him as a fine biblical scholar, whose teaching addressed social issues as well as doctrinal questions and was directed equally at the illiterate peasant and the thoughtful scholar. Antony's vocation as a preacher was so strong it gave rise to a legend that he preached to the fish one day when he was walking along the shore and had no human audience to hear him. His eloquence and the force of his message are suggested by the fact the fish are jumping out of the water to listen but his doleful companion looks much less impressed!

Antony is commemorated in the church which was built at Assisi to house St. Francis's remains because he was a Franciscan monk. Born in Portugal in 1195, he joined the Canons Regular but transferred to the newly founded Franciscans because of his desire to be a missionary. A spell in Morocco, working among the Moslems, ended when his health failed and he had to return to Italy. However, disappointment led to fulfilment, for his preaching and teaching ministry had a remarkable impact in the remaining years of his life. He died in Padua in 1231.

Antony, fourteenth century, Lower Basilica of San Francesco, Assisi, Italy

Elizabeth of Hungary

November 17/19

ELIZABETH WAS BORN in 1207, the daughter of King Andrew II of Hungary. A happy marriage to Ludwig IV of Thuringia ended prematurely when he died suddenly in 1227, on his way to join the sixth Crusade. A strong tradition held that she and her three children were turned out of the castle at Wartburg in the middle of winter by her brother-in-law. Traumatized in any case by the death of her husband, she arranged for her children's care, renounced the world, and became a Franciscan tertiary.

This was no sudden *volte-face*, for Elizabeth had always been devout and had long shown a tendency toward asceticism. She founded a hospice and worked so hard for the poor and needy that, careless of her own health, she died at the age of twenty-four.

Elizabeth became a very popular saint in Germany and is strikingly commemorated in thirteenth-century stained glass in Marburg Cathedral, but her reputation spread far and wide and has proved lasting, as is illustrated by this modern representation in an English parish church. This portrait highlights the gentle caring and spiritual sensitivity which have endeared her. A dog waits patiently at her feet, gazing up at her. While she is often depicted carrying a basket of food to represent her charity, here the abundance of roses which she holds symbolizes her desire to bring the fragrance of God's love into the lives of others.

Elizabeth of Hungary, 1938, Church of St. Mary, East Quantoxhead, Somerset, England

Julian of Norwich

May 8/13

ALTHOUGH SHE HAS never been formally made a saint, Julian (or Juliana) is remembered as one of the most inspiring of the English mystics and her *Revelations of Divine Love* is still read. Born about 1343, her original identity is not known because she probably took her name from St. Julian's Church at Norwich, in England, where she was a recluse, living under the Benedictine rule.

When, at the age of thirty, Julian became seriously ill, she prayed that her suffering would enable her to enter into Christ's Passion. In the Benedictine window at Norwich Cathedral, Moira Forsyth captures her cross-centered devotion and reflects Julian's recollection of her illness, when her curate said: "I have set the image of your Saviour before you; look at it and take comfort from it." As this portrayal of her face suggests, suffering brought a serene joy in God's love. She writes, "He is our clothing who wraps and enfolds us for love, embraces us and shelters us, surrounds us for his love which is so tender that he may never desert us." Such conviction is the basis for her famous saying: "All shall be well and all shall be well, and all manner of things shall be well." This is very close to Paul's saying, "All things work together for good for those who love God," (Rom. 8:28) but it is the intimacy of Julian's vision of God which makes her writings an enduring devotional guide.

Julian, *Moira Forsyth, 1964, Norwich Cathedral, England*

JOAN OF ARC

May 30

J OAN OF ARC, "the maid of Orleans," was a peasant girl from eastern France who, at the age of seventeen, responded to inner voices which she believed were a divine call to lead her country against their English foes. Having fallen into enemy hands, she was sentenced to death as a heretic by a politically biased church court and was burned at the stake at Rouen in 1431. Ironically, and not surprisingly, her execution severely damaged the position of the English, for she instantly became a symbol of resistance, which invigorated the French to shake off English domination. Joan was venerated in contemporary France as a patriot and military hero. By the time that she was formally recognized as a saint in this century, the perspective had changed and she was canonized for her integrity in following God's call.

In art Joan is always shown as a young girl in armor, with a sword, lance, or spear. Sometimes she looks very formidable, as she stands with sword drawn, ready to slay the foe, but this window, designed for a school chapel, makes her look very vulnerable and focuses on her spirituality. The sword is drawn but it is held like a staff, as Joan kneels in prayer, looking to God for inspiration. The golden fleurs-de-lys emblem of France is repeated, a reminder of Joan, patron of France.

Joan of Arc, Artist unknown, c.1952, formerly in the Grange Chapel,
Croft House School, Shillingstone, Dorset, England, now in storage but planned for use
in a memorial window in Holy Rood Church, Shillingstone

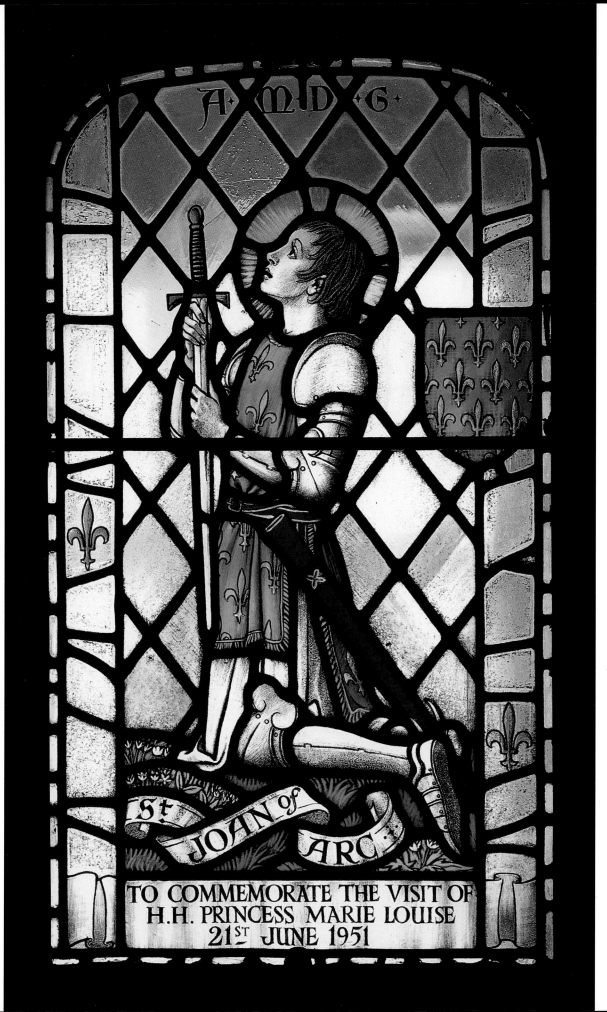

A · M · D · G ·

St JOAN of ARC

TO COMMEMORATE THE VISIT OF
H.H. PRINCESS MARIE LOUISE
21ST JUNE 1951

All Saints

November 1

ALL SAINTS IS a very important festival, for it is a day when we can give thanks for godly people whom we have known personally and for their influence on us. It is surprising there are so few windows representing All Saints, even in churches of that dedication. The theme offers a wonderful opportunity for an artist to portray ordinary people in familiar settings, but, presumably, the perceived difficulty arises in singling out individuals for inclusion among All Saints. A universal treatment could represent the homemaker who glorifies God in cheerful acceptance of daily drudgery, the carer who sees God in the handicapped child or aged Alzheimer victim—the list is endless and we shouldn't impose parameters.

I have chosen Michael, the archangel, to depict "the great multitude that no one could count, from every nation, from all tribes and peoples and languages, standing before the throne," worshiping God, along with the angels and elders, in the apocalyptic vision of Revelation 7. Michael is shown weighing the souls of the dead in a pair of scales, although, of course, it is God who judges. Human vulnerability in the face of God's judgement is suggested by the tiny, naked figure on the scales. Paradoxically, we are reminded that people who may seem insignificant to us, pass God's test of saintliness.

Michael, *fourteenth century, Church of St. Michael & All Saints, Eaton Bishop, Hereford, England*

Alban

June 20/22

ALBAN IS VENERATED as the first British martyr, but the date of his death is uncertain. A Romano-Briton living in third or fourth-century Verulamium, during a wave of imperial persecution of Christians, he was put to death for sheltering a fugitive priest. The great abbey of St. Alban in Hertfordshire, England, was erected on the site of his martyrdom and the name of the city changed in his honor.

Columba

June 9

BORN IN IRELAND about 521, Columba established on the Scottish island of Iona a monastery which greatly inspired the Irish church and spearheaded the evangelization of Scotland and northern England. A renowned scholar, he inspired generations of monks to copy the gospels. Thus the famous Book of Kells, written about 800, preserves a direct link for us to Columba. One of the great saints of Western Christianity, he died on Iona on June 9, 597.

Wenceslas

September 28

THE NATIONAL CZECH saint, more correctly known as Vaclav, is commemorated in the Christmas carol as "Good King Wenceslas." Born a prince of Bohemia in 907, during his boyhood his anti-Christian mother was regent but he was greatly influenced by his saintly grandmother, Ludmilla. When Wenceslas came to power in 922, he worked tirelessly to promote Christianity and peace, but his conciliation of his German neighbors led to his assassination in 929.

Stanislas

April 11

STANISLAS OF CRACOW, patron of Poland, is venerated as a saint who paid with his life for censuring an evil king. Born at Szczepanow in 1030, he became Bishop of Cracow in 1072. Little is known about his episcopacy, except that he boldly criticized and finally excommunicated Boleslav II for his scandalous behavior. Boleslav himself murdered Stanislas in 1079 as he was celebrating the Eucharist.

Hildegard

September 17

LONG REVERED BUT never formally recognized as a saint, Hildegard was one of the most outstanding women of medieval Europe. A leading figure in the twelfth-century church, she was abbess of the new Benedictine community at Bingen, Germany, from 1147 until her death in 1179. A theologian, political moralist, and visionary, Hildegard's views were sought and feared by popes and emperors alike. There is renewed interest in her as a composer.

Dominic

August 8

THE FOUNDER OF the Order of Preachers was born in Spain in 1170 and became a canon regular. Like Francis of Assisi, he founded the new order in reaction to the growing wealth and pomp of the church and the need for disciplined evangelism. From 1215 until his death in 1221 he led his "Dominican" monks in a simple, ascetic life, traveling tirelessly and giving priority to teaching and preaching.

Ignatius of Loyola
July 31

THE "PRAYER OF Ignatius of Loyola" is still very famous. A Basque noble born in 1491, Ignatius's desire to reform the Roman Catholic church in the face of the Reformation challenge led him to found the Society of Jesus. From the 1530s until his death in 1556, Ignatius oversaw the rapid spread of the Jesuits as teachers in universities and schools in Europe and in the distant mission field.

Teresa of Avila
October 15

TERESA OF AVILA is also famous for her prayer which begins, "Christ has no body on earth but yours." A sixteenth-century Spanish Carmelite, she matured from a dutiful nun into an inspired mystic, whose writings are devotional classics. She founded many reformed Carmelite communities throughout Spain, nurturing in each a disciplined life, with a balance between contemplation and purposeful action. Her influence was widespread for this new spirituality spread to the whole Carmelite movement, male and female.

Vincent de Paul

September 27

THE NAME OF Vincent de Paul, who was born in France in 1580, is known everywhere through the work of the lay charity founded in his memory in 1833. Vincent's priestly vocation was fulfilled in the service of the poor. The Congregation of the Mission (Vincentians) and the Sisters of Charity, which he founded to cater for the physical and spiritual needs of the people, still pursue his objectives worldwide.

Peter Claver

September 9

PETER CLAVER WAS a Catalan Jesuit missionary, who spent nearly forty years working in Colombia among the black slaves who were shipped there from West Africa. Distressed that South America's slave market inflicted unspeakable miseries on its victims, Peter dedicated his life to relieving their sufferings and defending their interests. Happy to consider himself "the slave of the negroes," he brought vast numbers of them to faith. He died in 1654.

Rose of Lima
August 23

ISABEL DE FLORES y del Oliva, known as Rose, was the first American-born person to be recognized as a saint. A Dominican tertiary born in Lima in 1586, she is regarded as the pioneer of social work in Peru and patron saint of South America.

Rose was a mystic, who practiced extreme asceticism to discover in her own experience the depths of Christ's suffering. After years of self-imposed deprivation and penance, she died in 1617.

Martin de Porres
November 3

THE SON OF a Spanish gentleman and an Indian or colored Panamanian woman, Martin de Porres is the patron saint of interracial harmony and justice. Born in Peru in 1579, as a young man he became a Dominican lay brother and spent his life working among the poor and sick of Lima. A man whose kindness extended to stray animals on the city's streets, he died there in 1639, particularly beloved of slaves and destitutes.

Kateri Tekakwitha
April 17

KATERI (CATHERINE) TEKAKWITHA is the first of three saints, who here represent the North American church, one a native American, one American-born and one a missionary to America. Kateri was the daughter of a Christian Algonquin mother and an Iroquois father, born in New York state in 1656. Orphaned at the age of four, under the influence of missionaries she became a committed Christian. Facing persecution by her people, she fled north to the Quebec French Mission and devoted the rest of her short life to prayer and service. She died in 1680.

Elizabeth Seton
January 4

BORN ELIZABETH BAYLEY in New York in 1774, before her marriage to William Seton, Elizabeth's faith led her to social work. One of the founders of the Society for the Relief of Poor Widows with Small Children in 1797, she was also a leading figure in the development of primary education. After the death of her husband, she converted from Anglicanism to Roman Catholicism and founded the first American order of nuns, the Sisters of Charity.

John Neumann
January 5

JOHN NEPOMUCENE NEUMANN was a Czech missionary to North America. In 1840 he joined the Redemptorists and rose to be their Superior in the United States. The founder of the Sisters of the Third Order of St. Francis and a pioneer of the American parochial school system, he was Bishop of Philadelphia from 1852 until his death in 1860. As bishop, he was renowned for his ministry to the poor, and as a preacher, educator, and church builder.

Teresa of Lisieux
October 1

TERESA'S BIOGRAPHICAL DETAILS are brief: Marie Françoise Thérèse Martin, born in France in 1873, entered the Carmelite convent at Lisieux in 1888, and died, after much suffering, of tuberculosis in 1897. However, her recollections, *The Story of a Soul*, had an enormous impact in the years after her death. It was, above all, her picture of the ordinary Christian attaining holiness by little daily acts of love that made this "Little Flower of Jesus" one of the most popular modern saints.

Maximilian Kolbe

and the Twentieth-Century Saints

MAXIMILIAN KOLBE IS one of the few twentieth-century Christians to be recognized as a "saint." His feast day is August 14, the date in 1941 when he died in the notorious Nazi concentration camp at Auschwitz. A Polish Franciscan priest, during the Second World War he sheltered Polish Jews and other refugees and challenged the Nazi regime in the Christian magazine he published. His inevitable arrest came in 1941 and he was soon transferred to Auschwitz. In July, in retaliation for the escape of a prisoner, the commandant ordered ten inmates to be starved to death in a cell. Maximilian volunteered in place of a married man who had a young family. His spirit was so strong he remained alive until all the others had died, encouraging them to pray and hold firm in the Lord.

There are many men and women whose lives and deaths were beacons of hope in the darkness of two world wars. Dietrich Bonhoeffer was a brilliant German theologian who returned from the safety of America to oppose Hitler in wartime Germany. Imprisoned for his part in the 1944 conspiracy against Hitler, he was hanged just before the end of the war. *The Cost of Discipleship*, and his *Letters and Papers from Prison* communicate his understanding of what it means to be a Christian in the twentieth century. Although Gladys Aylward survived the war, she certainly knew about the cost of discipleship. In 1940, as a missionary in Japanese-occupied China, she suffered terribly as she led some hundred children on a very dangerous trek to safety. That heroic journey took an enormous toll on her, but, undaunted, she continued her work.

There is a long list of Christians whose stand on injustice has led to their

The Last Judgement, *sixteenth century, Church of St. Mary, Fairford, Gloucestershire, England*

death. It includes Oscar Romero, Archbishop of San Salvador, defender of the poor and opponent of dictatorship, shot in 1980 as he celebrated the Eucharist, and Janani Luwum, Archbishop of Uganda, assassinated in 1977, after he spoke out against the tyranny of Idi Amin.

Thankfully, the twentieth-century saints are not all martyrs. Among inspirational writers is C. S. Lewis, remembered for such luminary books as *Mere Christianity* and *The Screwtape Letters*. Those who have devoted their lives to the service of the poor may be represented by Mother Teresa of Calcutta, and church leaders by Angelo Giuseppe Roncalli, who, as Pope John XXIII and architect of the second Vatican Council, shared a new vision of a worldwide and reunited Christian church.

Some are still alive and would resist strenuously any attempt to label them as "saints." Archbishops Trevor Huddleston and Desmond Tutu, tireless in the struggle against apartheid in South Africa, are but two of the many whose passionate commitment to God marks them out as remarkable Christians.

Bibliography

THE SAINTS
There is a very large number of books on the saints, including:
The Book of Saints, A Dictionary of Servants of God canonised by the Catholic Church, compiled
by the Benedictine monks of St Augustine's Abbey, Ramsgate,
6th edition, London, 1989.
The Penguin Dictionary of Saints, 2nd edition revised, London, 1983
The Oxford Book of Saints, 4th edition, Oxford & New York, 1997

CHRISTIAN CLASSICS
Many of the Christian classics are in editions other than those cited here.
American readers should note particularly the series,
The Classics of Western Spirituality, by the Paulist Press of New York.
On the Rule of Benedict, a very fine book by Esther de Waal, *Seeking God,*
London, 1984, clearly demonstrates its relevance today.

Augustine, *Confessions,* (ed. Gillian Clark) Cambridge & New York, 1995
The City of God, (trans. H. Bettenson) London, 1972, 1984
Bernard of Clairvaux, *On the Love of God,* (ed. G. Evans,& R. Payne) New York, 1987
Bonhoeffer, D., *The Cost of Discipleship,* London & New York, 1959
Letters and Papers from Prison, (ed. E. Bethge) London, 1971
Hildegard, *The Book of the rewards of life,* (transl. B.W. Hozeski) New York & Oxford, 1997
The text of Patrick's writings appears in *Patrick in His Own Words,* J. Duffy, Dublin, 1985
Secrets of God, writings of Hildegard of Bingen, (selected & transl. S. Flanagan)
Boston & London, 1996.
Lewis, C. S., *Mere Christianity,* London, 1983
Lewis, C. S., *The Screwtape Letters,* London, 1982
Teresa of Avila, *The Interior Castle,* London, 1986
The Collected Works of St. Teresa of Avila, (transl. K. Kavanaugh) Washington, 1976

STAINED GLASS
An excellent introduction is Lee, L., Seddon, G., & Stephens, F., *Stained Glass,*
London, 1976 & New Jersey, 1989

ON NINETEENTH-CENTURY ENGLISH STAINED GLASS
Harrison, M., *Victorian Stained Glass,* London, 1980
Many of the cathedrals and larger churches listed have guides to the stained
glass but there is a vast amount of research still to be done on nineteenth-century
glass and many windows are uncataloged.

The Youthful Francis Before the Bishop of Assisi, *fourteenth century, Kloster Kirche, Königsfelden,
near Zurich, Switzerland*

Acknowledgments

My thanks to Dr. David Edgar, New Testament lecturer in
Trinity College, Dublin, for advice on the biblical saints; to my
husband for reading the manuscript; to Mr. & Mrs. A. N. Moore for
proofreading; to the staff of the Library of the Representative
Church Body of the Church of Ireland for their help; and to
Dr. David Lawrence for sharing with me the fruits of his research on
stained glass in Irish churches, and for general advice.

Biblical quotations are from the *New Revised Standard Version,*
U.S.A.,1989, & G.B.,1993, copyright by the Division
of Christian Education of the National Council of the
Churches of Christ in the U.S.A.

John Betjeman's poem 'Christmas' comes from *A Few Late
Chrysanthemums,* London, 1954, and is reprinted in *The Best of
Betjeman* (ed. John Guest), London & New York, 1978.

Excerpts from the *Rule of St. Benedict* from the edition by
Timothy Fry, Collegeville, U.S.A., 1982.

Excerpts from *Revelations of Divine Love* by
Julian of Norwich from the Penguin edition, London, 1966, and
Showings (ed. E.Colledge & J.Walsh), New York, 1978.

The Editor would like to thank all who assisted in compiling this
book, especially the staff of Sonia Halliday Photographs, particularly
Polly Buston; the staff of Washington National Cathedral, particularly
Mrs. Vakey and Mr. Donovan; the staff of the libraries, archives, and
gift shops of Norwich Cathedral, Lincoln Cathedral, and King's
College Chapel, Cambridge; Dr. David Lawrence and Mrs. Meg
Lawrence; and The Rev. N. McConachie.

Victor, *Michael Healy, 1930, Church of St. Catherine and St. James, Dublin, Ireland*
Overleaf: The Ascension, *see title page*

TERBURY
HEDRAL

MIDDLE AGES

AM OF

FROM ADAM OF SAINT
VICTORS HYMN on the MAR-
TYRDOM of St CATHARINE

BEATA
CATHARINA
DOCTOS
VINCERET
DOCTRINA

VICTOR

S VICTOR